LOVE LIVES HERE, TOO

LOVE LIVES HERE, TOO

REAL-LIFE STORIES ABOUT PRISON MARRIAGES AND RELATIONSHIPS

The Think Outside the Cell Series

Edited by Sheila R. Rule and Marsha R. Rule

For information about this title or to order other books and/or electronic media,
contact the publisher:
Resilience Multimedia
511 Avenue of the Americas, Suite 525
New York, NY 10011
www.thinkoutsidethecell.org
877-267-2303

ISBN: 978-0-9791599-1-6
Printed in the United States of America
Cover and interior design: 1106 Design

Please note: The images used on the cover are being used for illustrative purposes
only. The persons depicted are models. (Photos: iStockPhoto.com)

In memory of William Rule,
our father,
whose heart was
filled with compassion

Contents

Contents

ACKNOWLEDGEMENTS

F IRST, I OFFER MY GRATITUDE and applause to the contributors, who by writing from their hearts will change the hearts of others.

My gratitude also goes to the Ford Foundation, without whose generous support this book and others in *The Think Outside the Cell Series* would not have been possible. I am particularly appreciative of the encouragement and progressive vision of one of the foundation's program officers, Calvin Sims.

Special thanks to the people in my longest-running relationships, whose life-sustaining love defies superlatives: my mother, Versa Rule; my sisters, Marsha and Diana; my nieces, Michaela and Alana; and, of course, my son, Sean, whose potential amazes me.

For her sharp editing skills and enthusiastic embrace of this project, my heartfelt thanks to Kathleen McElroy.

Finally, my heart sings praises to Joe, my husband, who transformed his life—and mine.

—*Sheila R. Rule*

I am deeply grateful to Sheila Rule and Joseph Robinson for their tremendous vision of creating a venue where the voices of the incarcerated and formerly incarcerated can be heard, again and again and again.

I want to thank the authors of this collection for the gift of their stories and for reminding me of the interconnectedness of all of our lives.

And, of course, my great appreciation to all the wonderful relationships in my life!

—*Marsha R. Rule*

INTRODUCTION

S TEREOTYPES. MYTHS. FEARS. These are the lenses through which Americans typically see the incarcerated, the formerly incarcerated, and their loved ones—when they see them at all.

More than 7.3 million people in the United States—or one in every thirty-one adults—are in prison or jail, or on parole or probation. Yet this population is largely ignored until a well-publicized crime by one person casts the wide net of demonization over them all. Tabloid headlines and reactionary scare tactics reduce anyone with incarceration in his or her background to a few dehumanizing descriptions—violent, hardened, menace to society, predator, heartless, unrepentant, and irredeemable, as in "once a criminal, always a criminal." And the people who love them are viewed as low-lifes, desperate,

1

or just plain crazy. The descriptions conspire to form a dramatic distortion, one that has created for these men, women, and families living in the shadow of prison persistent disadvantages and discrimination that few others in our society face. From employment and housing to voting rights and the everyday struggle to avoid being swallowed whole by poverty, the stigma of incarceration makes its weight felt.

But behind the stereotypes and myths, hearts beat and yearn, break and endure. Doubts, suspicions, and jealousies fester. Deaths are grieved and births are celebrated. Bonds shatter; wounds heal. Hopes are realized and dreams are trampled. Victories big and small stand alongside defeats of similar magnitude. Mistakes and bad choices are made. So, too, are wise decisions and hard-won transformations. Loneliness creeps here. Joy dances here. Love lives here, too.

Behind the stereotypes and myths, real people live.

One of the best hopes for bringing about a more realistic and balanced view of those living in the shadow of prison lies in having them raise their voices, tell their own stories, and speak their own truths about their lives. Over time, hearing their stories can lead the larger society to exchange stereotypes for names and faces, hear individual heartbeats, and witness nuanced lives. Hearing these stories can lead the larger society to discover that it is not "us" against "them," but simply "us."

And in telling their stories, the people of this forgotten population can inspire, encourage, and motivate those in similar situations. They can also begin to make greater sense of their own experiences, give expression to complex emotions, and gain a deeper understanding of themselves.

For these reasons, *Love Lives Here, Too: Real-Life Stories about Prison Marriages and Relationships* has been published. This anthology is a place where the incarcerated, the formerly incarcerated, and their loved ones have raised their voices and told their stories. It is a place where society can fully hear and see them.

The idea for this book had its roots in volunteer work that I began nearly a decade ago, after joining the Prison Ministry of the Riverside Church, a New York church internationally recognized for its commitment to social justice. I was asked to correspond with incarcerated men and women who wrote to the organization. And so I did.

Although generally dehumanized and demonized, the people I came to know through letters were multidimensional, complex human beings, like the rest of us. More than a few were skilled and talented in a range of disciplines, from art and music to sociology, business, and the law. And many had used their time in prison to rethink and disavow the values and belief systems that had brought them there.

The people I came to know were much greater than the bad choices they'd made. And they so inspired me that I would eventually found and devote myself to a publishing company that, as part of its mission, would seek to present a more balanced view of the incarcerated through books that would allow them a voice and help them tackle some of the hard challenges they face.

My husband, Joseph Robinson, helped to give definition and structure to my book idea. He suggested that I develop a series of books that portray the realities, gifts, and diversity of experiences of people with prison in their backgrounds. The series would take its name from the title of the book he wrote several years ago to help people currently or formerly in prison to use their innate gifts to build successful lives: *Think Outside the Cell: An Entrepreneur's Guide for the Incarcerated and Formerly Incarcerated*. Other books in the *Think Outside the Cell Series* include *Counting the Years: Real-Life Stories about Waiting for Loved Ones to Return Home from Prison* and *The Hard Journey Home: Real-Life Stories about Reentering Society after Incarceration*.

Contributors to *Love Lives Here, Too* tell their stories about marriages and relationships from various perspectives. Safiya E. Bandele, for example, reflects on time spent in a hospital prison ward with the man she's loved for many years, throughout his long incarceration: "It's surreal. This is the first time I've even seen him in a bed. It's the first time I've seen his toes (peeking from under the hospital cover) since we met on the IRT subway in Brooklyn, New York, in May 1969, when I noticed his beautiful feet in sandals."

A young contributor, Tanea Lunsford, recalls a childhood hiding the fact of her father's incarceration: "I never wanted to stand out by having to explain my situation. When we made cards for our fathers during summer camp or at school for Father's Day, I just made it and took it home without telling anyone I had no one there to give it to. The card would sit, unread, until the next time I cleaned my room, when I would throw it away."

Darrin Goldberg takes on the topic of this book in an unconventional way, letting readers in on his relationship with his dog named Regret: "'Can't you see I'm trying to get away with a crime?' I yelled at him. 'You're distracting me and bringing me unwanted attention with all that noise...' But... he kept barking and staring at me with his deep, penetrating eyes, as if he craved my attention."

Jason Dansby writes about the unbridled joy and frustration of becoming a new father while incarcerated: "My mind was racing on the way to the visiting room. I couldn't believe that I was about to meet my son. *My son!* I was actually responsible for something good in this world, something pure and wonderful. I could not wait to see him."

For Marlon Peterson, the topic of prison marriages and relationships brings up memories of the relationship he had with his brother: "He was never the big brother that would give his little brother the tough love most big brothers took pride in. Hell, there was no love...It would take years before I understood us."

In his story, Joel Williams, a writer in mid-life, honors "two guys in prison who've been my mentors in living, aging, and dying in prison. Huero and Mike didn't know it, but they were trainers for my soul. Their bare-knuckled bouts with pain and suffering taught me much."

I hope that *Love Lives Here, Too* teaches much. I hope that people who know prison's shadow find in these pages a reflection of their own unique personal power, and that they are encouraged to tell their own stories. I hope, too, that through these stories and others like them, the larger society comes to appreciate what those who know these men, women, and families already see—their inherent value and humanity.

—*Sheila R. Rule*
Publisher
Resilience Multimedia
September 2010

Tanea Lunsford

Hiding

HAVING AN INCARCERATED PARENT often means being part of a family where hiding the truth is a way of life. My first cover-up happened when I was two and my father was incarcerated. I noticed that he had not been around in a long time, and I asked my mother why. I had missed his scent passing by my room, an air of mystery always around him. At that age, I can't remember spending lots of time with him, but I remember wanting to. My mother, heartbroken by my constant inquiries, finally decided to tell me that he was "on vacation." I soon picked up the phrase, but I continued asking questions. I wanted to know when he would return. She could never give me an answer.

At the time of my father's incarceration, my mother was twenty-one years old, with a second daughter on the way. She did everything she could to transition seamlessly into a new life without my father, although it meant spending her prime party years supporting our household alone. At the time, she raised my sister and me strictly, but with more motherly love than one can imagine. In one moment she would scold us, putting us to shame with a shake of her head. In the next, she would share her bed with us as we tried our best to get closer to her, to feel her body warmth, her forgiveness. She took us to the park when she could, bought us pet fish, and always surprised us on Christmas.

Although she did not always show it, we knew our mother was lonely. When my father was first incarcerated, he and my mother divorced after separating on bad terms. My mother had never fully detached herself from my father, and the relationship (or lack thereof) made her noticeably depressed. My sister and I stopped asking about him because we saw the effect that the questions had on her attitude. My mother would often tell us that we were all she had. The judicial system had affected us all; it had separated us.

When I was about four, I found out that my father was not enjoying the beautiful beaches of Hawaii as I had imagined, but was living in a cold, damp cell. We visited him sometimes. Early on a Sunday morning we would stand in line for a long time behind what seemed like hundreds of women in heels and too much make-up and perfume, trying to make up for the circumstances, trying to cover up the sadness. They all looked so sorry.

My father was in and out of jail so much that sometimes we wouldn't know he had been out until we got a call saying that he was back in Folsom, San Quentin, or a county jail. I told myself that it didn't matter. I pushed it to the back of my brain and avoided conversations about fathers.

I never wanted to stand out by having to explain my situation. When we made cards for our fathers during summer camp or at school for Father's Day, I just made it and took it home without telling anyone I had no one there to give it to. The card would sit, unread, until the next time I cleaned my room, when I would throw it away.

It was not until I was eleven or twelve that my father was called upon to step up and do his job as a parent. My mother had been diagnosed with bipolar disorder and schizophrenia. The months before her diagnoses were confusing and scary for me. Unlike my dad, my mom had always been the stable one. Now, for the first time in my life, she was someone foreign to me.

She would lock her door and turn off her light—it was as if she wasn't home for months. I didn't know what was going on with my mom, but I knew it wasn't right. I tried to hide as much of the situation as I could from my little sister. I tried to protect her the way my mom had tried to protect me from my father's incarceration. When my mom locked herself in her room, I would tell my sister she was too tired from working to cook dinner, and I would make us Cup of Noodles. When my grandmother or aunts asked how my mom was doing, I honey-coated the situation to make everything sound fine. Instead of saying, "Mom won't let us drink the tap water. She says there is poison in it," I would say, "I got us a huge gallon of bottled water from the store. We like the taste better."

Watching my mother change was devastating, but covering it up came easy. After all, I had already spent years hiding the truth about my father.

After my mother's diagnoses, the truth could no longer be hidden. My sister and I saw her in a mental facility; we could not talk to her unsupervised. She was too thin—only two dress sizes bigger than my twelve-year-old frame—and looked sickly. A defeated look was always on her face.

My mother's condition was seen as potentially harmful to us and, because she had full custody, we were threatened with foster care. My father was fresh out of San Quentin State Prison again, and the court made an agreement that allowed him to be on probation for a shorter period and share custody of us with my grandmother.

We hadn't had much contact with him before this, only a couple of collect calls where, with the tone of a wanna-be hero in his voice, he asked what happened with my mom. He acted as if he wanted to save us, but when he was released, he was not much of a father. He still wanted to hang out as he had before. His irresponsibility led him to ask me for such favors as peeing in a cup for his probation officer so he wouldn't have to go back to jail. Even though he never said so, common sense told me that if he went back to jail, that meant foster care for my sister and me. So I did what I had to do, and he didn't go back to jail, not right away at least.

My mother was away from us for about six months, at one point living alone in an apartment a few miles from my grandma's house. We eventually had a group interview, and the caseworker found it appropriate for us to move in with her again.

Soon after, my father went back to jail—for the longest time yet. From what we have heard, his latest sentence is not coming to an end anytime soon. He may be rehabilitated this time. None of us will know until he gets out and stands on his own two feet.

But I know that I have definitely changed. Having my mom back home, I regained what was taken from me, and for that I am thankful. But I also learned from my mom's absence and my dad's not coming through as a parent that I could be independent. Once all the difficult truths were out in the open, I found that I had my own internal and spiritual resources, hope and determination, which pushed me to survive and thrive. I found strength in the things that made me fall the hardest—my parents' situations prepared me for the trials that might occur in real life and equipped me with ways to deal with them.

Now, at seventeen, I no longer worry about my father's incarceration. My energy lies in loving, forgiving, and succeeding, regardless of circumstance.

With medication, my mother has returned to her original state as my good ol' mom. She is having a baby now, another little girl.

My father has remarried and is still in San Quentin. Through our letters and collect calls, I am teaching him Spanish. We have our ups and downs, but regardless of what he has done, or will do, I am his daughter and no longer have a reason to avoid conversations about fathers.

I no longer feel as if I have to cover up for others. Because I know now that I am myself and not a shadow of anyone else.

Jason Dansby

Spitting Image

I T WAS A TYPICAL SUNDAY MORNING at the Southern State Correctional Facility, with life moving at its monotonous weekend pace. No mail. Education classes were closed. The entire place lacked motivation.

My alarm sounded when the clock struck 8:00. It was the most annoying sound to a man who cherished his slumber, but I knew that the alarm symbolized something greater. At 8:30 a.m., I was to see my wife, Patricia, who was pregnant. Those visits were a gift and a curse. Although I loved seeing her and hugging her in a time of such loneliness, I hated that she would leave crying, knowing that the next time we would see each other would not be until the same time a whole week later, if God permitted it.

I could not believe that I was away from Patty and my stepchildren—my family—when they needed me most. Dreams of being present during the birth, cutting the umbilical cord, and capturing every glorious moment of my first biological son's birth were always interrupted by the correctional officer yelling, "Lock in!" And every night, I had nightmares about the day I told my stepchildren that I had to go, and didn't know when I would be coming back. The nightmares would freeze-frame their reactions—hurt, despair, and confusion—and their sweet, innocent voices would cry out, "Why?" Seeing a parent locked up and not knowing why is a horrible thing when you are three or five years old. Trust me, I know. I went through the same thing with my mother, sitting in the holding cell of the police department in Hendersonville, N.C., and waiting for my grandparents to come and rescue me. It hurts knowing that I have put my children through the same agony.

I rose from my bunk. I had thirty minutes to get ready for my visit. I grabbed my towel, toothbrush, soap, shampoo, and washcloth. I slid into my flip-flops and made my way through the cellblock dayroom to the shower. If I had waited fifteen more minutes, I would have had to practically fight my way to the shower because of the rush of inmates getting ready for company, not taking "I was here first" for an answer. But for now, the dayroom was almost a ghost town, with only two other people around—the correctional officer and my homeboy G-Child.

I walked into the shower, placing my things on a plastic chair. I pressed the button, and out came the hardest downpour of water that anyone could endure. The water turned a few people away from actually taking showers, but when it was all said and done, they were forced to take showers by the other convicts in the cellblock. It was either wash yourself or fight. To me, showers represented a refreshing time. But no matter how rapidly the water sprayed, it could not wash off the guilt of being incarcerated while my other half counted the days until she gave birth to our son.

As I showered, I thought about the baby. What would we name him? Which one of us would he favor most? Would I be a good father? That question rang out in my head, followed by this one: How could I be a good father when I wasn't even there for his first breath? But I told myself that I couldn't think that way; if I continued that train of thought, I would go insane. I tried to regain what shred of dignity I had left so that I could face the woman I loved.

Fifteen minutes later the correctional officer's phone rang. He picked it up and spoke into the receiver. I could not hear what he was talking about, and did not care. After he hung up, I heard the officer's voice loud and clear, directed at me: "You don't have to worry about taking a shower. You're not getting a visit today." I thought he was joking so I started to wash my hair, when G-Child ran to the shower curtain.

"Patty's going into labor, Jay!" I could hear the panic in his voice. I could also hear the excitement. It was as if his own child were being born that day. My heart dropped into the nail of my big toe. I couldn't believe it. My son was on the way, and here I was, naked in the shower, with soap bubbles in my hair. I knew that I should be out calling Patty.

I rushed to put on my clothes and ran to my room to put my things down. I threw my shampoo and soap on my bed, but the shampoo rolled off and hit the ground. It woke my roommate, but I didn't care. My son was coming! My roommate could yell at me later; right now, I needed to get to a phone.

I picked up the receiver and started dialing frantically. I managed to get my inmate identification right on the first try, but I kept messing up when dialing my mother-in-law's house, where Patty and my stepchildren were staying. When I finally steadied my trembling hand enough to dial the right number, I waited excitedly for someone to answer.

The phone kept ringing, and I started to lose hope that anyone was there. I concluded that Patty had probably called from the hospital. Then, to my amazement, she picked up the phone.

"Hello?" Her voice was warm and soothing. Having had three children before this baby, she seemed to be handling the labor pains well. But just as I thought that, she said, "OW."

"Honey, I got your message," I said.

"Yeah," she said, delighted. "Your son is on his way."

It was a miracle! God had blessed our family with a baby boy. God had blessed the pregnancy, and it was now time for our baby to meet the world.

Soon, every word Patty spoke ended with "OW!" The contractions were coming closer and closer. Her breathing became heavy.

"You're gonna do just fine," I assured her. I knew that I was not in a place to be of much help, but I could calm her by talking until she had to go to the hospital. I wanted her to know that I was going to be thinking about them—as if I wasn't always thinking about them.

"I wish that you were here."

When she said those words, I started to cry. I felt the same way. I started to feel downright mortified that I was missing this moment. Thoughts ran through my head: Will he hate me for missing this day? How will I tell him? But I couldn't let my insecurity overshadow this day. I wouldn't allow it to happen.

The 'Ows' became more primal, more intense. She needed to get to the hospital.

"Sweetheart, you've got to go!" As much as I didn't want to end our conversation, I had to.

"You know that I won't be able to make it to visit?" she asked me sarcastically. I smiled. It felt good knowing that, even at a time like this, she could still be funny.

"I know, sweetie. Now go have our angel." It hurt saying those words. I wanted to be with her that day. I couldn't get over that fact, no matter how I tried.

She said she'd probably have him before our visit that day would have been over. And then, with a voice drained and depleted, she asked, "What do you want to name him?"

I drew a blank. For so long, Patty and I had our sights set on a baby girl, and then we were told that it would be a boy. I didn't know what I wanted to name him, but I knew that I wanted it to be special. I wanted it to be something that he could look at and know that his father loved him dearly. Then it came to me.

"Let's name him Dejaun Ahrian Dansby."

I don't know where I came up with that name, but I knew it was the name for our son. I thought about it—Dejaun Ahrian

Dansby. It was a cute name, but the initials said it all: DAD. I was very happy with my choice, and I knew Patty was, too.

It was March 14, a week later. I did not bother to get up and shower because I knew that Patty was not going to come so soon after giving birth, that she was probably still hurting from the delivery. As for me, I wanted to sleep the week away so that I could possibly see my son the following week. I had continued to call Patty while she was in the hospital. The prison superintendent had allowed me free phone calls. In one of those calls, I heard my son start to whimper, and I cried tears of joy and pride. My boy was here!

At 8:30 a.m. the phone rang at the correctional officer's desk; after a few minutes, he hung up the phone and started to yell off the names of people who had visits. At the end of the list, he yelled "Dansby!"

My wife had come to see me. I hoped that she'd brought our son.

I jumped out of my bunk as fast as I could and brushed my teeth. I didn't have time for a shower, so I washed up as best I could. I threw on my prison-issued uniform and ran out of the room.

My mind was racing on the way to the visiting room. I couldn't believe that I was about to meet my son. *My son!* I was actually responsible for something good in this world, something pure and wonderful. I could not wait to see him. I wanted to see what he looked like. I hoped that he would be awake so I could see his eyes. I wanted him to see me. I wanted him to know that his father loved him. I wanted to kiss him on his forehead, and to assure him that I would be home soon.

I pressed the first door that led to the corridor to the visiting room. I walked down the corridor. With every step, my heart beat a little harder, a little faster. I walked to the visiting room door and looked through the window. I saw Patty sitting there, holding what seemed like a bundle of blankets.

I walked into the room and over to my wife. She was holding our son with a beautiful smile on her face. She had a radiant glow about her. The blanket lay over Dejaun's face. I looked down at the blanket and back to Patty. I had such an enormous grin on my face. I could not control my emotions. At first I was smiling. Then, Patty grabbed the side of the blanket masking our son from the world and pulled it back, revealing the biggest, most beautiful brown eyes I had ever laid eyes on. He was awake and staring at me! His eyelids batted so perfectly, like the flutter of a beautiful monarch butterfly floating magnificently on a breeze during a pleasant summer day.

At that moment, I wept tears of bliss. How could I have helped create something so precious, so perfect? Patty looked at me with delight as she held the baby, thanking me for helping to create him. Then she raised him in the air, asked me to hold him, and gently placed my first-born son in my arms.

I looked him in his eyes. I could see his purity and love when I gazed into them. His small nostrils quivered with every breath he took. He was the perfect addition to an imperfect world.

I placed my hand on his tiny hand, which was making a fist. His grip loosened and he slowly latched onto my large index finger with fascination. I caressed his tiny hand as he continued to hold my finger. Then, suddenly, his mouth opened, letting a long-deserved yawn escape. Dejaun, my son, was tired.

Patty retrieved a bottle from the bag that she had carried into the visiting room and handed it to me. I placed it in his mouth, and felt his little lips tug on the nipple as he drank the contents of the bottle. I remained fascinated throughout the entire process. Then his tug became lighter and lighter until it was no more. My baby boy was fast asleep.

Dejaun is now five years old, very smart and the spitting image of me. He has settled into his own identity and has become quite a big boy. He has a lot of my traits—like taking baths instead of showers and loving Oreo cookies. But who doesn't love Oreos? He has my facial expressions; he thinks his flatulence is hilarious. Okay, Okay. I admit I used to find humor in that, too, when I was his age. I think it's comical. But, he knows better than to do it in public.

Unfortunately, I have not been able to spend a holiday with him. His birthdays are spent with his brothers, sister, mother, her boyfriend, and family. His Christmases are filled with presents that his mother, aunts, uncle, and grandparents have bought him. His mother buys presents and tells him that his daddy told Santa to give them to him. Even though his mother and I are no longer together, I will always respect her and love her for that.

I make my contribution by working with programs that supply gifts to children of the incarcerated so that they know that their fathers are thinking about them.

Having two older brothers, one older sister, one younger brother, and a baby sister on the way, Dejaun has etched his place among his siblings and is a dominant force among them. That must be the Dansby in him. The children are as thick as thieves and love each other dearly.

For years, I have recorded myself reading books. I send the books and tapes to Dejaun and the other children so that they can hear my voice. To this day, Dejaun brags about how his father reads to him before he goes to bed, and how his father loves him. I talk to him on the phone, and he continues to ask if he can stay with me at "school." I always have to turn down that request.

To some, I am a convict. To others, I am a caring and loving individual. To everyone, I am a mere mortal. But to the little man that I speak of in this story, I am a legend. I am a hero. I am Superman.

Stacy L. Burnett

I Smile

T ODAY MAY BE THE DAY I see my son. Three hundred and forty-seven days—nearly half his lifetime—have slipped by since we've seen each other. I wake an hour before sunrise and scurry into the shower while my world is quiet. The soft lather of minty apple soap, steaming spray, and blessed silence feel more like home than prison.

The reverie never lasts. The telltale dip in the water pressure and curse-laden banter remind me I am number 09G0379, I live in Cube 35 in Dorm 121-A at the Bedford Hills Correctional Facility, and I must not linger if I want first dibs on the hairdryer.

Toweling off completely is not a luxury I afford myself this morning. Once I belt my state-issued felt robe, I pad over near the sleeping officer, place my prison ID card in the slot where the dryer is kept, and carefully remove the implement without waking him. Hairspray is forbidden, so I massage the approved hair gel into my roots. Ponytails are the only hairstyle sanctioned by the Department of Correctional Services. Normally I pull my hair into an elastic band and don't worry when the ends don't flip up. But today is not normal. It will be the best day of my incarceration—my son may visit—so I trade the dryer for the curling iron. The barrel is smaller than I prefer, but the results are adequate. By the time 121-A is summoned to the mess hall, it is raining. So I skip breakfast to preserve the curls I coaxed into the ponytail.

It was from Kathy's last letter that I learned that I might see my son today. Kathy was a relatively new friend—she barely knew me and had never met my son—when she agreed to help out and plucked him out of foster care. She provides thorough updates about his progress. Whenever those updates arrive, they already feel like old news, but I devour each detail, buoyed by each stride he's made. "Yay! He's stringing words together!" If I digest those details for too long, I sink with the realization, "Grrr! He mastered that long before foster care!"

Kathy lives forty-five minutes or so from this facility. The postmark on this latest letter indicated that she mailed it on Monday; I should have received it Tuesday or Wednesday but only got it last night—Friday. This weekend is Mother's Day, and it is tough to feel good about being a mom when I'm reading a letter from someone who has to change my kid's diapers. I don't want the reminder of all my maternal failings leaping off the paper with the mention of all the skills he is relearning. But then, on the fourth page, in her scrawling letters, Kathy wrote, "1.0 is taking Matthew for the weekend, and he is supposed to bring him to visit you."

My son, Matthew, is named for his father. Neither of his other boys bears his name; he mentioned to me once that his wife felt "one Matt was enough." I don't mind the name, but I eschew "Junior," and adding "the second" to any name just seems too lofty. To provide Matt the delight of a namesake, our son's name is punctuated with 2.0, like a software upgrade. His name shouts, "Here I am—the improved version!" To keep the two Matts straight, "Big Matt" is 1.0 and Matthew is 2.0 for those in the know.

Visiting hours in Bedford are 8:30 a.m. to 3:30 p.m., seven days a week. I am not going to the gym or the yard in case my son comes early. I hover around the officer's desk so he won't have to track me down—if today is the day 1.0 brings my son. My workout partners notice that I skipped breakfast and that my hair is curled when I miss Denise Austin's Jazzercise video. They return at 11:00 and notice that I am sitting in the same chair, and am on the same page of my *New Yorker* magazine. They whisper, "He isn't coming; he would've been here by now," or "Traffic on 684 always sucks," or "He got here too late and couldn't get in." Someone counters, "Everyone knows it's always packed on Mother's Day."

The Jazzercise crowd abandons me for the showers, and it dawns on me that 1.0 has Matthew because his wife probably jetted off to Colorado with their children, leaving him to sneak in quality time with the byproduct of our affair. I know this because I have spent two Mother's Day weekends with him under precisely these circumstances. And then I know there will be no early start to this day with his girlfriend, Julie, skulking around.

The bile inside me builds as I imagine her pillow talk: "Poor baby. At least your son has *you!* You are such a good man, going into that place for *her.*" I halt the conversation in my mind, knowing it ends with a comment about the great kid and how I do not deserve him.

The officer calls my name. I have a visit. My son is here.

Dorm 121-A is located on the opposite side of the prison and is the farthest point from the visitors center. The unit officer writes me a fifteen-minute pass at 11:50 a.m. Ten of those minutes are not needed. My sneakers are still wet, so I am wearing the state-issued boots that do not fit and make my toes bleed; but they are clean. An officer must search me before the visit to ensure I am not smuggling anything out of the facility. She did not anticipate my prompt arrival and is smoking. If my feet were not burning already, I would be pacing. How long does it take to finish a cigarette? I want to shout. Don't these people understand they are stealing time from my visit? A whole year crammed into three hours—that is a lot of pressure. I wait. I smile.

My son is on the other side of this wall. While I wait, I envision the toddler who relishes the rumble of passing trains and chucking bits of chicken on the floor. Oh, how the dog waited for him to grow restless at the dinner table! Sand was a hundred pounds of canine terror to those he did not like (almost everyone), but he was second only to me in the fierce loyalty and love department where Matthew was concerned.

He invented games for Matthew, too. Mostly Matthew stood in place while Sand darted around him like a sheepdog hemming in his flock.

On the other side of this wall is the little boy stomping his feet and giggling in my memory, his downy tufts of dark blond baby fuzz bouncing. That ended 347 days ago, too.

Menthol hangs heavy in the air. I guess the officer inhaled the entire carton during her break. She barks orders at me; the first is to take off one boot. I hand it over for inspection, as I think about the squalor that once encroached on the clean spaces of our house ("Other boot, please!"), as depression sapped the will from my body. ("Give me your socks!") I think about how I stopped caring when 2.0 splashed the contents of Sand's bowls all over the house. Or when the garbage piled up on the front porch. ("Open your mouth!") Circumstances rendered me an automaton. ("Put on those boots and stand up!") But I was bereft of proper programming and subsequent support. I squeezed Matthew so tight and let everything else slip through my hands. ("Arms out!") And, then, he was gone.

I enter the visiting room. Sitting atop his father's shoulders, Matthew has the most expansive view in the room. I wonder if Matthew is nearsighted, and the first twinge of panic hits me when there is no attempt made to slide down his father and crash into my legs. Big Matt points to me; Matthew points to the vending machines.

"He's just hungry," Matt says.

I smile, though I think it is odd that an experienced father, cradling his fourth child, traipses out of the house without feeding him first. Matt digs through his wallet and fishes out a small bill to buy a single-serve bag of white cheddar popcorn. Vending machines and handling money are prohibited for prisoners, so I sit in the cheap plastic chair at table #49. Big Matt coaxes Matthew to sit in the chair next to me, using the voice parents save for persuading reluctant children to swallow medicine that looks and tastes like bug juice. He opens the bag for 2.0, and I leap into action. I know this boy and the imminent disaster presented when he is granted unfettered access to quantities of food. I hope the floor is not carpeted with popcorn before I return to table #49 with paper towels and wipes.

It isn't. I am amazed; 347 days ago, Matthew would have been climbing on the table and kernels would have been flying out of the bag, a popcorn cyclone! Today, he reaches into the shiny foil sack, takes a single puff of white cheddary goodness and plops it into his mouth. Once completely chewed, the kernel is swallowed, and the process is repeated. Who traded my son for a circus pony? Matt is muttering something about discipline and manners. I know Kathy has worked hard to effect these little miracles. What really troubles me is the way Matthew eyeballs me in between each gentlemanly bite, and then his eyes search his father for clues. My heart scrapes against sandpaper as the gritty truth unfurls at table #49.

My son does not recognize me. He does not know I am his mother.

Running around, laughing, and blowing raspberries against his smooth, perfect skin do not ignite a spark of recognition. His father patiently interprets the words I do not understand—which are most of them. 2.0 plops a toy in his father's lap and reaches for Matt's hand (not mine) when he spies the playground. Matt holds the door for me, #09G0379, the interloper in this father-son adventure.

Under the circumstances, Matthew's indifference may be a blessing. I deserve much worse for all he's endured on his own. He moved four times, each requiring an adjustment to new people, different smells, routines, and meals. He lost the house he knew, filled with his toys, his pets, and the Kit Kat hiding spots that entertained him for hours. As soon as he found one, he raced to me, extending the orange package as a peace offering. Once unwrapped, he snatched it back and ran off to a dog-free zone to eat it in privacy—the only snack he was loathe to share.

What happened to all his memories? Has he written over the first half because it was all so terrible? How is it possible every cell in his body does not recognize our biological connection? I sit and watch a boy I knew dribble a basketball, run up a slide, and push open doors. My heart is more scratchy when he walks past me, whispers to his dad, and then Matt announces a pretzel mission. They run off to the vending machines and I lag behind, smiling as my heart and toes throb with each forward motion.

Ninety minutes into the visit, 2.0 discovers the toys in the children's center. I steer him toward the low tables and kiddie chairs so we can make some cards. A volunteer digs out some paper and bits of broken crayon mashed into a numbered Styrofoam cup. Tomorrow it would be nice for him to give Kathy a Mother's Day card. If he'll sit still long enough, maybe we can finagle a few extra that I can squirrel away and mail out to Matt and Pop Pop on Father's Day. Another zinger. I realize I've never received a Mother's Day card. Last year, Matt said he bought one for me, but it doesn't count because I've never seen it. 2.0 does not want to do anything artsy. He runs off, and I can't catch him. The volunteer snatches the unused paper from the table and locks away the cup of crayons.

Matt and I sit side by side, our legs stretched out straight in front of us. I cannot remember if I kissed him or he kissed me, but I do remember the old thrill that used to ignite every neuron from the top of my head, down my spine, resulting in toe-curling bliss. My heart and feet must be too sore to dance. I feel nothing.

"I filed for divorce."

"How does it feel?" I ask.

"Good."

"Then, I am happy for you."

We hold hands while he recounts the lurid details, avoiding any, I notice, that could circle the conversation around to his girlfriend, Julie. There must be a reason he is telling me this now. He's written me numerous times in the four months since these events occurred. We do this routine, this game where we pretend we do not see the giant crater in front of us, even when we both know it is there. I can relax, finally, because the territory finally (finally!) looks like the version I recall. My heart recognizes his attempt to be kind, affirming my belief that he is a good man. It is too bad I turned out screwy. We could've been great together.

There is nothing for me to do with our son right now. I want Matt to sit 2.0 down and trace the stubby fingers on yellowed paper so I can hold his hand after he leaves. I want to pound on his chest until he understands these minutes evaporating between us are boiling down all the hard truths I live with, and the answers I need aren't "Forget about it," or "Don't worry." Maybe there aren't any answers, and I am just afraid the questions hanging over that gaping hole will deepen the rift. But my son is happy, his father looks right, and I smile.

The visiting room is emptying, and my resolve to remain cheerful is cracking. It is time to leave, but Matt is not respond-ing to my suggestions that he should beat the crowd out. He counters by telling me there are forty-five minutes left. Our son is tired, and I understand clearly the implications of tir-ing out a child so adults can squeeze in some private time on a predictable schedule. In 347 days, Matt has sailed on and Matthew has found a lifeboat with Kathy, while I am sifting through the flotsam and jetsam of a shipwreck.

I am losing the fight against my urge to grab my son, to hug him, and to keep kissing all that creamy baby skin until he is soaked and my lips are parched. Only I can't force love on a stranger, and do not want to frighten him because I am scared to death.

Matt chooses now to tell me he filed a custody motion. He is angry that Matthew watches NASCAR races with Kathy's family and falls asleep in the shadow of cartoons every night. I decide against reminding him about the last foster home, where Matthew cried himself to exhaustion but seldom to sleep. Kathy is a good mother to our son; most of the children of my fellow prisoners aren't so lucky. I decide to wait for the papers to come so Matt can hang onto all that self-righteous indignation a little longer.

The humiliation of the strip search does not sting as bad as the revelations in the past three hours. My socks are bright red where the boots chafed and tore my skin. The officer runs her gloved hand over the raw spots as though she is scrubbing a stain, feverishly trying to rub it out before it sets. She apologizes, and I realize I am crying. My toes will hurt tomorrow. It is my heart aching now, but I just wait for her to finish. I sit back in the chair and picture my son with a Kit Kat, chasing his dog.

And, I smile. I see my son.

Marlon Peterson

My Brother's First Kiss

"...because love covers over a multitude of sins."
—*1 Peter 4:8 (New World Translation)*

W E WOULD PASS EACH OTHER on the street like total strangers. No words exchanged, not a smile. A perfunctory nod of the head was the extent of our greeting—not even a change in walking pace to acknowledge each other. We lived together in a one-bedroom apartment in Brooklyn, along with our parents, our older sister, and her son.

That stranger was Mikey, my older brother by eight years. My brother was definitely not my keeper. Mikey never spoke to me, at least not about anything significant. There was the occasional "you talk too much," or "your lips are too big," but never a conversation about important things like girls, basketball, and the latest sneakers—nothing brothers would usually share. He was never the big brother that would give his little brother the tough love most big brothers took pride in. Hell, there was no love.

It was as if he was ashamed of me, or maybe jealous of me, or plain old hated me. It would take years before I understood us.

I felt the shame, or hatred—or both—the summer when I was about eleven. On my way to the park by myself, bouncing my basketball, I spotted Mikey, our cousin Kurt, and another guy standing together on an adjacent corner. Kurt saw me from across the street and called me over.

"Marlon, where you goin'?" Kurt quizzed.

"To the park."

The friend interjected, "Yo, who is Shorty?"

"That's Mikey's little brother," Kurt volunteered.

"I ain't know Mikey had a brother," the friend said, as if a long-buried secret had just been revealed. He turned to Mikey to interrogate him.

"I've known you all these years. Why you never said that you had a brother? Why I ain't never seen him? Damn, you got him going to the park by himself?"

"Man, shut up!" Mikey reprimanded. "He don't like hanging out with me."

A complete lie.

Amazingly, he told this lie without placing an eye on me—as if I wasn't standing there and able to refute his scathing excuse for hurting me. Furthermore, how could I not like hanging out with him if he never gave me an opportunity?

Dejected, I left the three and walked my ball to the park four blocks away.

Mikey adored our nephew DJ, who was nine years my junior. He would pinch DJ on the neck in the affectionate way I'd seen him do with my sister.

Was I the plague, a leper, the carrier of a contagious disease? Was I not a cool enough little brother?

I began to hate him so much that I began telling my friends that I only had a sister because to say that I had a brother was akin to lying. I was bankrupt of any brotherly stories.

Nevertheless, there were times when I would try to befriend him despite our sister's advice to accept that he didn't want anything to do with me.

"Mikey, can I go to the park with you?"

"No, get out of my face!" he would say, shattering my heart like a 1,001-piece jigsaw puzzle hitting the floor just before the last piece is put in its right place.

"Mikey, you wanna play me in basketball on Nintendo?"

"No, go play by yourself."

Why did he hate me so much? Was it my fault that I was the baby of the family (until DJ was born)? Was it my fault that he was sent to live with my grandparents in Trinidad for the first five years of his life? Was it my fault that our parents were too broke to raise him *and* my sister? Was it my fault that our parents were in better shape financially when I was born, affording me small luxuries that they could not afford when he was a child?

Was it my fault?

At nineteen years old I was still looking for an answer, and an older brother, but in the wrong place—the streets. Two weeks before my twentieth birthday I was arrested for my role as a lookout in a botched robbery that resulted in the senseless deaths of two innocent people. Not surprisingly, all of my co-defendants were older—surrogate big brothers without the sincerity of brotherhood.

Then it happened, two and a half years later, with me remanded without bail, still awaiting trial and facing a life sentence. It was not under the best of circumstances, but beggars can't be choosey.

Mikey was visiting me in a jail visiting room in Queens, New York. The one-hour visit—a rare one from him—was ending. I was dressed in a short-sleeved jumpsuit with D.O.C. (Department of Corrections) posted on the back in big white stencil and a long strip of Velcro for a zipper on the front of the suit. I wore rubber slippers with white socks.

Mikey was now an inch shorter than me at 6'1", but still more muscular. The chairs and tables were the perfect size for preschoolers. Our table was next to a window where the Saturday morning sun provided a solar spotlight. Most of the other visitors filling the room were wives, girlfriends, and infants. Men rarely visited men in prison. Yet here sat my brother and I catching up on our present because we did not have much of a past to discuss.

"Your visits are now over. Visitors, please make your way to the exit," a female voice rudely interrupted over the annoyingly loud and muffled speakers.

"I'll speak to you later, Mikey, a'ight," I recited without eye contact, turning to walk back to the area where we, the incarcerated men, were to return.

Then it happened.

My brother grabbed me by my left arm gently, spun me toward him like a scene out of a 1950s romance film, and kissed me on my right cheek, simultaneously pinching my neck.

He said, "I love you. Call me tonight."

"I will, and I love you, too," I replied.

Right then, all those years of mutual animosity and hostility, all those moments of humiliation, rejection, dejection, all those years of malignant emotional battering, all those memories of hate were extinguished with that one gesture.

And all it took was a kiss—a brother's first kiss. A testament that no matter how long it takes and where it takes place, "love [always] covers a multitude of sins."

Mikey, you are the brother I have always wanted.

Daniel Skalla

Bite the Wax Tadpole

I PUT MY FINGER IN THE WATER RINGS left on the table by the people who sat here before. Still cold from their sodas. I wanted one myself. My mouth was dry. My mind was going over the words I wanted to say. I knew I would not say them as well as I could think them.

I wiped up the water, the faint lines of the water rings still visible. Just a memory of what had been here before. Wadding up the wet paper towel in my hand, a drop of water slipped out. I thought how something so soft and refreshing could erode a mountain to nothing. Kind of like what the lack of communication does to destroy the relationships we share. Destroy the bonds we share.

I shook my head. Please, I thought to myself, I don't want that. I felt as if the voice in my head was screaming. As if there was no one to come to the rescue to save me from this world of make-up and make believe. Walls and fences. No defenses. No resolutions.

It's not that I was afraid to say what needed to be said. But would she understand what I was trying to say, or look at me with dull interest like a well-fed cat lying in the sun, too tired to be interested in chasing the everlasting, dangling string?

I saw her behind the glass as the guard with the buzz-cut let her in. I wondered if she felt violated being searched on the way in, his hands on her body. She looked around and came over. She sat across from me, and we made talk that was small, going back to those times in life that were more care than free. She would have been smoking a cigarette, carelessly flicking the ashes on the clean table, if she were allowed to smoke at all. She couldn't, not here.

"I'm sorry I don't write," she said.

"That's OK; I understand."

"I've just been too busy."

"I know; I'm sure it isn't easy," I said.

There was a pause in the conversation—like the bad part of a good movie or like waiting too long in the supermarket line. I shifted on the hard chair trying to get comfortable, but comfort was not an option.

"I miss you," I said.

She looked away.

Silence.

"Do you want something to drink while I'm still here?"

"Sure," I said, as I watched her handle the change that I was not allowed to touch.

I watched her walk away.

She came back and set the can very near where the round water ring had been. I took a drink. Coke. After seventeen years with her. I don't like Coke. Never did. At least not this kind.

She said nothing.

"How is work going?" I asked.

"Fine, I guess."

She looked empty, tired, older.

The pangs of guilt ripped through me. I wanted my lifestyle. I caused pain and suffering. I never had the desire to make the right choices. I never fulfilled my responsibilities as a parent, a spouse, a son, as an employee, as a man. I wasn't there when I was there, and I'm gone now. For a long time. They nailed my ass to the wall. I caused so much damage and pain. I hate it. I hate me.

"When are you leaving?" I asked her, my voice empty, my mind numb.

"Soon; I need to get going."

"That's not what I meant," I said. Did I really want to go there?

"I'm sorry," I said.

She looked up and I realized the hollow emptiness of a phrase so worn that it didn't mean anything, even when it meant everything. I leaned back and asked her, "So what are you going to do?"

"I don't know, I just don't feel the same way about you anymore."

"I understand."

She looked up, and I looked her in the eye. It was the first eye contact we had made since she walked in.

"You were never there for me when I needed you; in fact, you were never there at all. Self-absorbed in your little bubble." Her voice cracked. "I know what I did wasn't right, but he paid attention to me. I get lonely. He's good with the kids."

A pain formed deep in my heart. "I wanted our family to be a family again," I said.

"I want to move on. It's time. I gave you enough chances and look where you are now. I hope you're proud of yourself." Her voice shook with anger.

"I'm sorry about the drugs." I sat empty. "I did the best I could."

"Bullshit," she said, her voice rising.

The guard looked our way, looking for that subtle indiscretion. Any infraction would terminate the visit. He was on it. I looked away.

God forsake the uncomfortable silence. What good were words?

She started speaking slowly. "You did what you wanted, and it hurt. You hurt the children; you hurt me. What the hell were you thinking? Why didn't you quit? All your friends quit years ago, but, oh no, not you."

"I didn't think I could," I said, grasping for excuses that would cover years of turmoil and suffering. Typical.

"Bullshit. You made choices; you made your decisions; you made your excuses. We live with the consequences."

The sound of her chair dragging on the floor was like a steel door slamming shut on a life that we would never see again. The end of the future.

She walked out. I was struck by how beautiful she really is. After all this time. After living the hard life. She deserved more, something better. I guess I hoped it would be with me. I was wrong. Could I have given her a better life? I don't think I could have if I wanted to.

A deep sadness wrapped around my chest. I kept thinking about the communication that was lost all those days we spent not talking, next to each other, slowly evolving through the course of life. Much like a river finding its own way in spite of what the earthen boundaries suggest. Waking up one day with someone you don't even know. Someone you've spent your life with. Someone you didn't share your life with. Those times of silence and misunderstanding. The ensuing bitterness and regret.

I leaned back and smiled. Bite the wax tadpole.

My inner stream of conversation took me back to an article I read about Coca-Cola. When they marketed their product in China, the Chinese characters that were used to spell their name also read as "Bite the Wax Tadpole." Nobody caught the idiosyncrasy in the translation. I know how they feel. I tried to say what I meant, but it all came out wrong. I know what I meant to say, but it's not always what the other person hears. Sometimes I am able to articulate my thoughts, and comprehension and understanding abound. Then there are those times when my head and my heart are disconnected, nothing works and, in frustration, I settle for an anguished silence.

As I stood to leave, I threw my half-empty can in the trash. I smiled a tired smile, thinking of the billboards in Beijing with a man holding a Coke in one hand, a big smile on his face, and the words "Bite the Wax Tadpole" over his head.

Preston Seville

Fighting Temptations

I MET MY WIFE, SHA, at a Garth Brooks concert in Central Park. The first thing everyone usually says when I tell that story is, "What the hell were you doing at a Garth Brooks concert?"

No matter. Sha is a gorgeous, brown-skinned woman of Trinidadian descent, with almond brown eyes. At 5'8" and 150 pounds, she has a Coca-Cola bottle shape. When I first saw her, I was mesmerized.

Not long into our relationship, I went through a long, drawn-out trial, and I was convicted of two armed robberies. No one was killed, but I received the maximum sentence permitted: two consecutive twenty-five-year sentences, a total of fifty years. I was twenty-two years old. Sha sat through the entire four-week trial, weeping a silent monsoon.

We were not yet married, and I told her to live her life without me. I considered it an act of unselfishness, but perhaps it was a deep-seated fear of being rejected. But Sha refused to leave. We've now been together almost twelve years. In that time, amid the stressful environment of prison, my love and passion for her have left me constantly thinking of her needs, wants, and desires.

Countless times, in person or over the phone, she has expressed her fears and aspirations, and her dreams of the day when we will finally reunite outside this madhouse. Her fears are profound and frighteningly familiar; her dreams are nutrients essential to my growth; her aspirations a symphony of melodies that I dance to.

❧❧❧

"Count time, count time, on the standing count," blurts a broken-down PA system, interrupting my dreams about Sha and snatching me back to reality. Our circumstances are grim. She is discouraged by her relatives, who believe she could and should be doing better. Her friends are temptations; they plant seeds of negativity.

"Sha, he might be a homo-thug…" "Love ain't got nothing to do with it, nor can it pay the bills!" An endless barrage of "You know what I heard?" And the worst of all: "Have you seen that show on HBO, 'Oz' ?"

The negative perceptions from her peers, her family, and the media become overwhelming. Adding insult to injury are the stories about the men who, when released from prison, fail to do the right thing by their women. All the loyalty, dedication, faithfulness, dreams, and sacrifices of these women are trashed, shattered, and discarded. It's disgusting.

During Sha's sacred time of the month, a flood of hormones persuades her to question and analyze everything. And when the moon is full and the tides change, so do her perceptions. "Do you truly love me?" "Why do you love me?" "How can I be sure you'll remain the same man when you come home?" "What about that chick who wrote you last year?"

I can only respond from my heart, and make sure that my actions are consistent.

Each conjugal visit, I try to reassure her. For forty-four hours (2,640 minutes), Sha and I laugh, vibe, pray and meditate, feed one another, share our deepest emotions, cry, and make spiritual love. For 2,640 minutes, she has my undivided attention. She has no reason to assume that she isn't my queen, no reason to believe there is another. I give her undiluted appreciation; I compliment her dedication and reciprocate her sacrifices tenfold. Whether she knows it or not, I have been and continue to be faithful to her. It is disheartening to watch my wife depart at the end of the visit. But I'm helpless in this situation.

There are, of course, my own insecurities. Being in prison has a way of compounding trivial matters, and manipulating insecurities. Like many others in my circumstances, I have found myself constantly worrying about whether tomorrow will be the last day. Tomorrow, she could wake up and suddenly decide "Enough is enough!" I silently pray that she doesn't allow another man to take my place. Will she abandon me, leaving me bitter, wounded, angrier, miserable, brokenhearted?

I struggle with these thoughts and images as I toss and turn on a thin, sticky, uncomfortable plastic green mattress.

I tune into KISS-FM and listen to Lenny Green soothing and charming the women who call in. I wish I'd hear my wife call in, dedicating one of our favorite songs to me. These are just hot-air-balloon dreams. But I have to remain positive and keep hope alive. Otherwise, I'll be just like those prisoners who end up in a psych ward, medicated up on Thorazine, looking for cigarette butts in the rain.

I love my wife; I love my son, who's from a previous relationship. If I could do it all over again, I would not have picked up that red bandana, the guns. I would not have been involved in crack dealing, marijuana smoking, and womanizing. I have made a decision that I can be different and change my life for my wife, for those I love—and for myself.

I could always go backward again if I chose to, but Sha encourages me to step outside the box. Reality—the concrete walls and the thick metal bars that encase me—often threatens to overpower my optimistic mood. I fight to remain positive and try to convince myself that everything is all right. Isn't God good? Aren't all of the Creator's favorites tested? Job was tested. My ego and id argue amongst themselves. My mood changes quickly. Am I exhibiting symptoms of bipolar disorder? Or, possibly worse, post-traumatic stress/slavery disorder? I can't help but laugh out loud at my personal satirical play.

Sha's voice often resonates through the madness that clouds my vision. "Baby, you have to think for both of us now." "You should have thought about that shit before we got married!" "Baby, you have to trust that you'll be here soon." Once again, she saves me from slipping through the cracks into institutionalization or insanity.

I awake with new vigor. I'm revitalized for another day of monotonous activities. I refocus on things that will guarantee a future for Sha and me. I take, excel in, and complete all vocational programs and training. I continue studying for my bachelor's degree in human services, complete my Department of Health certifications, and complete my Department of Labor certification as an HIV/AIDS counselor. I am determined to change. I will create a means of employment. I will create a means for survival. I cannot return to a life in the streets. There are no second chances for me. I have to move my pawns strategically.

I return from the yard one day to find a piece of mail on my floor. It is a letter from my father, whom I haven't heard from in seventeen years. He tells me he was just released from prison, blah…blah…blah. I cannot see or comprehend anything else—my anger and frustration toward him won't allow me to. I chuck the letter behind my bed. The song "Heard It All Before" plays through my mental radio.

In April 2008, my fourteen-year-old son was arrested. He was publicly crucified and charged with manslaughter in the accidental death of a college student. I was devastated, but I saw it coming. I warned my sister that she should keep a closer eye on him. She would scream in anger, "What do you want me to do? The boy is bad; he doesn't listen."

My family didn't help matters by emphasizing to him, "You're just like your father—a liar, a criminal; you just can't behave!" I believe this pushed him further into the streets.

Although my son had free will, no one seemed to guide him; no one seemed willing to present him with alternatives. They only screamed, hollered, and told him what he could not do. No one took the time to show him how to accomplish his dreams.

I wrote to my son and spoke with him by telephone weekly, but he was mad that I wasn't there with him. Just as I was mad that my father wasn't with me when I was growing up. On a few occasions, my son would say that he wanted to come be with me in prison, or he would ask how he could get me out. I would subtly suggest positive ways for him to help me. "I need you to go to school to be a lawyer." "I need you to get your education, secure a good job with the right amount of money so we can buy my way out."

I was aware that he was beating up people, and even robbing them. I told him it was wrong. I genuinely think he knew it was wrong, but he wanted to impress his friends. He wanted to prove that he was tough or a gangster—like his father. My so-called associates would see my son and tell him about all the vicious things I had done in the streets, and he made every attempt to emulate me.

When my son was arrested, he was interrogated by the same detectives who arrested me; they convinced him to sign a statement. "Don't be like your dad," they told him. "He was sentenced to all that time because he refused to tell on his associates." This made my blood boil. But I was saddened that a person had died at the hands of my son. I wrote a letter to the court sending my condolences, but I never received a response.

Just as my father and I became statistics, now my son was caught in a terrible cycle that our patriarchal history is insistent upon repeating. Without question, Sha was affected.

Even though my frustrations affected my attitude and disposition, I had to try to not pull her in too deep. She was experiencing enough stress and strain, with two of her brothers and me in prison. As a teenager, when I trained as a lifeguard, one of the first things they taught us was to be very careful when trying to save someone who was drowning. They could very easily drown you with them. I had to be careful not to drown Sha while she was making every effort to save me.

"C1-234, Seville, legal mail," the PA system announces. My heart beats faster; my pulse quickens. I hand my prison ID over to the legal mail officer and sign at the designated location. The cop inspects the contents of the letter and envelope for contraband. I'm finally handed my mail. I briskly walk away. I read through the letter's procedural jargon. I skip through the pages and go to the back, where it's either stamped "granted" or "denied."

Damn, there it is: "Motion Denied."

My brain bursts into a million different voices. I am disappointed and know Sha will be, too. When should I tell her? Should I tell her at all? I decide to wait until our next visit.

I dread having to explain the complicated appeals process and another disappointment. But when I do tell her on a visit, we agree to return to the drawing board. The remainder of our visit is filled with laughter, setting priorities, and enjoying each other's presence.

I recall how Sha and I used to walk through Riverside Park. The moon's glow reflected off the still water into a kaleidoscope of colors. It was absolutely beautiful. We slowly strode along the water's edge. I miss those free moments of peace so much, moments when we weren't racing against Father Time. On our conjugal visits, we attempted to replay these memories, but it wasn't the same. We always found ourselves racing against the clock.

The reality is that we are in a long-distance relationship. Sha tells associates and co-workers that her husband works out of state. Her friends who know the truth can't understand how she can make the sacrifices she makes. I, too, sometimes wonder how and why she does. Would I do the same for her if the shoe were on the other foot? It is a question I hope she never asks, and one I cannot wholeheartedly answer.

Sha and I will probably never understand what the other endures, but one thing is certain—we have molded our relationship to overcome practically any hurdle.

We go through the same things that couples on the outside go through. We make up to break up; fuss, bicker and fight; agree to disagree and then join forces; love and make love. So what's the difference? A magnitude. After prolonged states of denial and intense bouts of rationalization, I must admit there are major glitches in our relationship—the body searches, visit procedures, prison atmosphere, societal attitudes, discouragement, awkward stares, and a long list of misconceptions.

However, our relationship is based on communication, trust, and honesty. Without these three components, we would not have made it this far. We recognize that any problem—when well-expressed with honesty and empathy and handled with compromise and courtesy—can be overcome. There is no fear of being judged, ridiculed, or rejected by the other; expressions are clear and concise; opinions are respected and analyzed.

We will always be better than some and worse than others. Tomorrow isn't promised, so we live for today. I find myself using the Narcotics Anonymous phrase, "One day at a time." Once we master the present, it equips us to accept the past, and keeps us looking forward to the future.

"Seville, 222, mail on your gate."

I'm rudely interrupted from slumber. I retrieve four pieces of mail from the cold metal bars. One is from my mother, the second from my son, the third from Excelsior College, and the fourth is from Sha. I can smell her sweet, seductive perfume before I see the address on the envelope.

I read Sha's letter first. She seems frustrated about the incarceration of her brother. I contemplate my response; the last thing I need is for her to become more frustrated trying to stay strong for her brothers and me. I decide to let my thoughts marinate before answering her letter.

I begin to read my mother's letter, which is slightly difficult because she is a deaf mute and writes with odd grammar. She writes her letter as though nothing has happened, as if two and a half years haven't passed since I last heard from her. I feel as if she's abandoned me, but I have to realize that I abandoned her and my family by coming to prison. I am her oldest child and only son.

"Would she rather see me dead?" I'd ask Sha. "Don't say that," she'd respond with a scowl.

I read the letter from my son with particular interest. He's incarcerated at a youth camp. He seems to be all right and is mostly staying out of trouble, minus a few fistfights. I write him back and tell him all the things I wish my father had told me. I hope that something somehow sinks into his head and makes him consider the causes and effects of his thoughts and actions.

At the end of the night, I place Sha's letter beside my pillow. As I drift off to sleep, she's right by my side. I miss her and look forward to our next conversation, our next visit, our next trailer.

Or, will there be another?

Joseph Robinson

Five Words That Renewed My Marriage

WHEN I ASKED SHEILA TO MARRY ME, I knew that our lives would forever be different. More complex. More challenging. And more devoted. It would not be easy. But I was certain that taking the big step would be well worth all the ups and downs we'd experience as a married couple.

Sheila and I "met" in August 2002. I'd written to the Riverside Church Prison Ministry seeking a pen pal. I'd also hoped to find a companion—someone with whom I could share my dreams and my pain, someone with whom I could engage in stimulating conversation, someone who could help me stay in touch with my humanity after a decade in prison. I received a response from Sheila Rule, the Prison Ministry volunteer responsible for corresponding with the incarcerated.

In her naturally sweet way, she basically told me that there were no "young" women in the Prison Ministry and that its members would continue to fight for justice and fairness for me and other incarcerated people. Her card reminded me that I had absentmindedly used the adjective "young" in my letter to describe the type of companion/pen pal I was hoping to meet. I immediately wrote back to her, explaining that my use of "young" was casual, a cliché, not meant to be taken literally. Then, in the span of six or seven pages, I shared my hopes and dreams for myself and for my son, Joseph, who was then twelve years old.

Sheila responded that she could not be my companion but could be my friend. After we began exchanging letters, my life went from black and white to Technicolor. I became more engaged with the world. I had more hope, a greater sense of purpose. As months went by, I fell in love with Sheila's heart, compassion, sharp intellect, and genuineness. She fell in love with me, too. We were married on January 25, 2005, at Sullivan Correctional Facility in New York, surrounded by my mother (who had travelled from North Carolina) and my son, Joseph, along with Sheila's son, Sean, and our dear family friend, Rose.

Sheila and I couldn't stop beaming at each other as we sat with our cheerful and supportive loved ones in the prison visiting room. We were like two grownup kids, giddy and filled with electric energy that we had no idea what to do with.

"So, how do you feel, Joe?" Rose asked as she smiled like a proud mother. "Do you feel any different?"

It was a bit surreal. Now that I was officially a married man, a husband, I didn't know how to articulate my overflowing joy. I had a lovely wife. I was the happiest man in the world. I was on Cloud Nine.

All eyes were on me. "I feel great!" I said. "It hasn't totally settled in that I'm now a husband, but I am." Laughter danced around our two small tables.

"And you, Sheila?" Rose asked. My new wife, as beautiful as could be, patted her bosom. "I feel honored. I feel honored."

I reached for Sheila's hand, held it tightly, then leaned over and kissed her on the lips.

My mother, not known for being shy, then asked, "So when are you two going to be able to...you know, be a husband and wife? Consummate your marriage?"

I blushed in embarrassment. *No she didn't! No my mother didn't just ask me, in front of my wife and two boys, when we would be able to make love!* But indeed she had. And she looked at me, and then Sheila, waiting for a response. That's just how my mom rolls. Straight, no chaser. I love that about her.

I told her that it would be approximately six months before we'd have our first conjugal visit. My mom thought that was too long. So did Sheila and I, but there was nothing we could do. Under Department of Correctional Services rules, we had to be married for ninety days before even applying for the Family Reunion Program, as the conjugal visiting program is known. Then it would take another two to four months for the approval process to take its course.

As we waited, our letters, phone calls, and regular visits taught us more about each other as individuals and as a new couple. Our love for each other deepened by the day. We'd never had so much as one argument or disagreement. And we couldn't imagine having any.

Before we knew it, we were preparing a list of meals for our first two-day conjugal visit. It was July 2005. I will never forget those first days and nights spent alone with Sheila. Uninterrupted conversations. Delicious food. Exquisite lovemaking.

Sheila and I quickly got the swing of the conjugal visits. Every ninety days or so we got to experience these extended periods together. We'd come up with creative and fun ways to make each "vacation" different. We'd plan activities around a particular theme, or if a notable event or milestone was approaching, we'd plan to celebrate it. Each conjugal visit transplanted us from the prison grounds to wherever our fancy took us.

When my book, *Think Outside the Cell: An Entrepreneur's Guide for the Incarcerated and Formerly Incarcerated,* was published in 2007, we celebrated by having a mock publication ceremony. Using the back of a black fake leather sofa as a rostrum, Sheila gave me a stirring introduction that spoke of my accomplishments, the man I had fashioned myself into, and the legacy I was destined to leave. She then called me up to the "stage," from where I thanked her for her gracious introduction and thanked my imaginary audience for supporting my efforts.

Like all marriages, our rosy, seemingly unblemished union was tested. How else were we to learn that ours is indeed resilient, consistent, and reliable? Less than a year into our marriage, my son, Joseph, presented the first major test. He argued and fought regularly with his maternal grandmother, with whom he lived, along with two cousins, in a tiny apartment in the Brooklyn projects. He stopped going to school. The year Sheila and I got married, he ran away at least eight times. Each time, Sheila would get a call from the police saying that Joseph had given them her name and would she pick him up. She always did—traveling to New Jersey, to the northern edge of Manhattan, to downtown Brooklyn.

But as much as Sheila loved Joseph and accepted him as her own son, she was taken for a loop by his chaotic life. It was just the opposite of the quiet, comfortably predictable life she'd led with Sean for the past twelve years. For me, the chaos underscored how I could not be as present in my boy's life as I longed to be. For a while, it seemed as if all of my telephone conversations with Sheila began and ended with her reports of the latest mess that Joseph had gotten himself into. She was trying to be helpful, to include me in what was going on. But after a while, I started steeling myself as I approached the phone to call Sheila; a part of me dreaded the conversations. I started viewing her as the messenger of bad news. And I found myself growing quiet during our conversations, as I tried to process whatever had happened next and how I could help. Sheila took my silence as a sign that I was withdrawing from her.

One afternoon, Sheila visited me unexpectedly. Since we routinely plan our visiting days, it scared the hell out of me. I immediately noticed her uneasy smile when I entered the visiting room. She looked haggard, exhausted.

"What's the matter, Sugah?" I asked, as I leaned over the table and planted a kiss on her cheek. I sat down beside her.

Sheila took a deep breath. "I'm fine. I'm fine."

But her eyes were heavy with concern. I grabbed her hand in mine. "What's the matter?" I repeated.

She had been visiting Sean at his school farther upstate and decided to see me on her drive home. She told me that she was worried that she wasn't doing enough to help Joseph—to rescue him from his unhealthy environment, to rescue him from himself.

She also worried that Joseph was coming between us.

I offered reassurances, which allowed me to speak to my own emotions. It helped us both, I think.

"Listen, Sugah, you're doing everything you can for Joseph," I said. "And I really appreciate all that you do in my stead. It hurts my heart that he's going through all of this stuff. It saddens me that his mother died so young, that she can't take care of him the way he deserves. It doesn't help that I've been in prison since he was two years old. This shit is hard."

Sheila nodded her head. She understood and was glad I did, too.

The next two years found us continuing to struggle with how to help Joseph. But it also found us humming along comfortably in our marriage. We had a nice routine, part of which included carving out time to watch Dr. Phil, Tyra, and Oprah on our conjugal visits. Depending on the topic, the shows often provided material for rich discussions in which we would learn more about ourselves and each other, discussions that would last long after the programs were over. In January 2007, we listened to a marriage expert on "Oprah" talk about the importance of couples having periodic conversations about how their marriage was doing. The guest suggested a simple exercise: each person should choose five words to describe the marriage.

Sheila and I glanced at each other from opposite ends of the futon. We knew that this exercise had our names written on it. Sheila came up with these words to describe our marriage: healthy, focused, striving, growing, working. I saw our marriage as supportive, nourishing, healthy, wholesome, and enriching. We were in good shape, a testament to our commitment to making our marriage work. The exercise would become an annual ritual; in our first conjugal visit of each year, we would write down five words that best described the state of our marriage. We'd read aloud the words we chose, then elaborate on why we had chosen them.

Two months later, I decided to write *Think Outside the Cell*, a combination self-help and entrepreneurship book for the incarcerated and formerly incarcerated. I was a born entrepreneur and, in the years I'd been in prison, I'd read every personal finance and business book I could get my hands on. I even traded cigarettes for books in order to build my own business library. Word spread among fellow incarcerated men that I could help them with personal finance issues and business-related questions, and I soon became the authoritative advisor on such matters. In 1995, I began formally teaching personal finance and entrepreneurship classes, which I continue to teach to this day.

I wrote the book in the spirit of giving back, of making a difference, of leaving a positive legacy. I wanted to encourage people currently or formerly in prison to use their innate entrepreneurial gifts to build better lives and break the brutal cycle of recidivism. As the manuscript took shape, and as I developed a marketing plan for the book, I felt my entrepreneurial wings spread. No longer were my days squelched by the monotony of prison life. I felt a renewed sense of purpose. I was on a mission to provide hope and direction to the hopeless and directionless. In the process, I was determined to show the world, to prove to my family—and to myself—that I had transcended prison. I was determined to prove that I am not my mistakes, I am not my past.

Sheila and I decided that it would be best for the book to be published by the publishing company she'd founded about a year earlier as a way to give a voice to the incarcerated, the formerly incarcerated, and their loved ones. I was excited; I knew that I could serve as an expert advisor through the process. But before long, our vastly different approaches surfaced. They created tension in—and at times overwhelmed—our marriage.

With her decades-long experience as a newspaper journalist, Sheila was used to operating solo, keeping ideas close to her vest, working things out for herself. She's an introvert.

I'm more of an extrovert. I liked to talk up my projects, bounce them off others. Networking and reaching out for assistance came naturally to me. It made business sense. Plus, in prison you either seek help from the outside world or wither away into obsolescence.

She found business to be more intimidating than she first thought when she started her company—she stepped into entrepreneurship with faith and passion, more than anything else—and her approach was to plod step by step. Meanwhile, I was the idea person, quick off the mark, impatient and passionate. She exercised a lot more patience than I ever could, but she procrastinated whenever she felt in over her head.

I was in my element, having been raised in the rough-and-tumble streets of East New York, Brooklyn, and having had a taste of street entrepreneurship. Sheila worked best by focusing on one thing at a time. She was more detail-oriented than I, and preferred to complete one task before embarking on a new one. I needed to always be mentally engaged—perhaps to combat the monotony that stifled the air and the people around me. I sometimes needed to work on several projects at a time to feel fully engaged, to feel a sense of movement and progress.

Our differences began to take on a life of their own. We sometimes struggled to maintain a balance between our marriage and her publishing company. I would nag Sheila or complain about how she didn't think or operate like an entrepreneur. And I'd "advise" her on being more effective, more productive—as I saw it, as I understood things.

Sheila would shut down, feeling inept and overwhelmed. "I'm not a natural entrepreneur, Joe. You are. I'm a writer. That's what I'm good at," she'd remind me. I understood this on an intellectual level. But since I couldn't run her business and could only serve as an advisor, I pushed her to get up to speed. Since I couldn't be on the outside to help execute our marketing plans, I pushed her to do the things I couldn't do. I couldn't attend business seminars and workshops. I couldn't network and participate in social networking sites. Sheila could do all of those things. And more. But, as far as I was concerned, she didn't know where to begin or how to proceed. And she wasn't comfortable asking for help.

On some level, I began to resent Sheila. Our letters, telephone conversations, regular visiting room visits, and even our conjugal visits were marked by the ebb and flow of oppressive stress and determined resilience. Sheila would remind me that our marriage made the business work—not the other way around. She'd express concern that we talked about business more than our marriage. She was right, of course, but each time she pointed this out, I'd grow silent in anger and frustration, my entrepreneurial wings continually clipped.

The strain of the business—and the differences in our styles that it highlighted—was reflected in our choice of "marriage" words for the next two years. On January 25, 2008, our third wedding anniversary, I described our marriage as hopeful, optimistic, challenging, rewarding, and enriching. Sheila described it as striving, challenging, evolving, resilient, and hopeful. Clearly, we were placing bets that our marriage was as hopeful and resilient as it had been in the past, and that we remained pretty much in good shape. But the word "challenging" on both our lists spoke to the marital strain that was in the air.

By far, 2008 was the toughest year of our marriage. It wasn't unusual for Sheila and me to grow silent on the phone—when we're angry at each other, we tend not to raise our voices but to inject long stretches of dead air in our conversations—and to sign off with a quick and perfunctory "Love you." We were experiencing more stress than joy, more heaviness than lightness.

The words we chose to describe our marriage on February 4, 2009, were telling. They sounded an alarm. Sheila saw our marriage as evolving, complicated, serious, frustrating, and striving. I saw it as challenging, a work-in-progress, transitioning, complicated, and heavy.

What a change from just two years earlier. I had even been reluctant to do the five-word exercise, but I knew it was important.

After explaining to each other why we had chosen our words, we stared into each other's eyes. In Sheila's, I saw pain and sorrow. I also saw a determination to make our marriage work.

"Wow," was all that I could initially utter. After a moment, I said, "We've got to do better than this, Sheila. We've got to do better."

Sheila nodded. "Yes; we've got to do better. And we *will* do better."

It was a sobering moment. We had somehow lost the joy and lightness that once typified our marriage. We had to renew our commitment to our vows and each other. We had to renew our marriage.

A major breakthrough occurred when, during one of our Sunday morning telephone conversations, Sheila and I came to understand that we were complicit in the problems we'd been having. We realized that we'd been trying to do the impossible.

"Sheila, it just dawned on me that for the past two years, I have unconsciously tried to live through you," I said. "I've been trying to make *you* do what *I* want to do. That's what's been going on all this time. I cannot live through you."

She was quiet at first, as if mulling over my words.

"Given your circumstances, and your dreams, gifts and passion for entrepreneurship and making a difference, it's understandable how you'd try to live through me," she finally said. "But you're right; you cannot live through me. And now that I think about it, I know that I have been trying to rescue you. On some level, I have been trying to help you live through me, so that you can realize all of your dreams, live some semblance of the life you want. The bottom line is that I can't rescue you any more than you can live through me."

That telephone conversation—a week or two after our last conjugal visit and five-word exercise—was a turning point. No longer did I nag Sheila about how differently we operated, about how she should carry out a task one way or another.

I began emphasizing that we needed to talk more about us, about our marriage, about our hopes, dreams, and plans as a couple. Business had its place but, as Sheila had said time and again, it was our marriage that made everything else work.

We established pre-determined days and times to discuss marital, family, and business topics during our telephone conversations. We incorporated the use of a whiteboard to plan and complete weekly projects. We laughed more often, and we expressed our love and appreciation for each other even more frequently.

Our commitment to do better, to having the marriage we want and deserve, has paid off. Sheila and I have grown closer by the day. As she likes to put it, "we're an old married couple." While we are careful not to become complacent, we are humbled and grateful for the wonderful marriage that God has blessed us with.

On February 17, 2010, we again took the pulse of our marriage. Sheila described it as sturdy, resilient, evolving, supportive, and working. I described it as balanced, familiar, working, promising, and routine. We are indeed an old married couple, comfortably nestled in our marital nook.

As an addendum, I'd like to add five words to my standard set: I love you, Sheila Rule.

Vickie Nelson

It Was a Good Day (or So I Thought)

I CE CUBE'S JOINT "It Was a Good Day" reflected my state of mind on the morning of Friday, January 18, 2002. I was leaving Nashville, heading south on I-24 to Murfreesboro, Tennessee. The Rutherford County Detention Center was my destination, which for the past year and some change had been my husband's humble abode.

This trip, however, was different. This would be the last time that I would travel to some prison, Big House, county jail, or some deep-in-the-country correctional facility. No more waiting for some correctional officer to say "That's enough" while I was kissing and hugging my husband. No more sitting in a chair marked "visitor," facing my husband as I spanked him in a table-slamming game of Spades, Tonk or UNO.

The days of the early-morning stops at the carwash to get $10 worth of quarters to feed a prison vending machine for its selection of unhealthy zoo zoos, wham whams, hot wings, and M&Ms were soon to be long gone. My husband was coming home.

The forty-five-minute drive back to Nashville was filled with excitement and anticipation for both the "physical reunion" and our rich future. All I could think of was the beautiful, happy life I'd share with this sexy, dark-skinned, bald, buff brother who reminded me of Scarface of The Geto Boys—and who was now "chillaxin" in the passenger seat of my Chevrolet Suburban.

After all the jail terms my husband had served and all the years I'd spent as a lonely wife patiently waiting for my "man" to come home, I felt extremely vindicated, for some reason. Vindicated is a strange term to use, but that's exactly how I felt. Before his release, well-meaning friends and family had lovingly suggested that I leave him; they'd said that I should move on because of all he'd put me through.

When I picked him up that day, I just wanted to call everybody up and say, "See, I told you so."

Once we got home, our day was filled with erotic kisses and passionate hugs. Things were amazingly perfect, and I was happy to be his wifey. I thanked God.

And that amazingly perfect day led to a very special night. After "knowing" one another (biblically speaking), I'd cooked his favorite meal—fried chicken thighs with Hunt's tomato ketchup on the side.

When he came home, my husband was every woman's dream. I was a queen decked out in a bejeweled crown, seated next to my boo on his throne. He was attentive and loving. He rubbed my feet and my back. He even went grocery shopping with me—not one of his favorite things to do, but he willingly did it.

Things were great that day and the next day and the next—and then something went wrong.

After that first week of bliss, an all-too-familiar reality surfaced. My husband began to morph back into the brother that I'd hoped had been lost in the abyss.

His release from jail had been conditional. He'd been placed on intensive probation, which meant that every night for three months he'd have to be in the house by 6:00 p.m. My husband, the street hustler that he was, felt this "situation" was just a little too confining for him to abide by, that it justified his defiance. Life was moving in slow motion for him; having to be cooped up in his crib from 6:00 p.m. to 7:00 a.m. for the next ninety days would somehow diminish his swag.

The streets had missed him and were now calling. It started with a late-night card game at a friend's house the weekend after he was released. A party at the house of one of his boys came next. That house party proved to be the beginning of the end of my blissful week—and led to his quick return to the pokey.

The more I tried to reason with him—"Look, dude, you only have ninety days; it won't kill you to stay at home, *and* you promised the judge"—the more he convinced himself and tried to convince me that he would not violate probation. He "thought-jacked" my misguided belief that his future would be better than his past and that "three hots and a cot" would never again be his reality.

Four months later, he succumbed to his chosen bondage. He was soon equipped with XXL county blues stamped with TDOC—for Tennessee Department of Correction—and a pair of white K-Swiss, size twelve. He had been arrested on drug and weapons charges and would serve about two-and-a-half years of an eight-year sentence before he was released on parole.

So much for my happily ever after, huh?

My husband was released from the Whiteville Correctional Facility on April 27, 2005. Exactly three months later, on July 27 at around 7:00 p.m., I received a call from the Davidson County Justice Center. It was my better half.

"Hey, baby. Man, I'm sorry, man."

"For what, Steven?"

"I'm in jail, man."

"What did you do, Steven?"

"Man, they set me up. Look, Vick, go get that money and come get me out before they 'violate' me!"

Hours earlier, my husband sold a ridiculous amount of narcotics to an undercover vice officer at a local motel. Before I could bond him out, he'd been "violated" by his parole officer.

This time, he served about three years before being released on parole on April 11, 2008.

The many years of dealing with a man who had his own agenda and his own concept of marriage took a damaging toll on our relationship. My husband was a hustler, and the streets were his home. This dead-on fact was obvious to many, but I was seemingly oblivious to it.

I did find it odd that my husband, who was such a loving, beautiful man behind bars, would hardly come home after being released each time. But I made excuses for his behavior and rationalized his inappropriate actions as just being a "man thing."

My husband was a provider, financially. He made sure that the bills were paid. If I needed an extra $200 here or $500 there, he'd get it to me. He felt that as long as he made sure the bills were paid, he'd done his part. This financial support played a major role in my staying in an unfulfilling marriage.

For years, I'd listened to my husband promise me that "this would be the last time." I had such strong faith in him that I neglected my faith in God. I trusted my husband to change even after I'd realized that he would never change.

The truth was that my husband was a repeat offender three times over. He'd spent so much time behind bars that when people would see him on the streets, the first thing they'd say was, "How long you gonna be out? When are you going back?"

His stints with freedom were just borrowed time.

More often than not, we were dealing with forced separations that are part of every prison relationship. This type of separation comes with often irreparable situations: the seemingly justified infidelities, the missed birthdays and holidays, the strain on the bank account when a main provider is absent, the insurmountable number of opportunities that fade away—to travel the world together, to raise a family together, to start a business together. This separation is the reason behind many taxing collect phone calls that begin with "Why did you do this to me?" and end with "I can't do this anymore!"

Innocent children ask consistently, worriedly, "Where is my daddy?" or "Where is my mommy?"—only to be misled with the infamous tender and protective response, "On vacation, baby."

The prison separation causes other problems, too. God positioned men and women with a sexual desire for the opposite sex, but when this moral right "by design" is taken away from a man, it brings about a desperation that can lead to "getting some" by any means necessary.

Once, my husband was within two months of being released from his eight-year term when, on one of my visits with him, he snuck into the women's restroom and sent for me. I was scared to death of getting caught, but I was more upset that he'd risked his upcoming freedom for a few moments of pleasure. "You could have waited," I said with clinched lips. "What is wrong with you? Why would you chance not getting out by doing something so irrational?"

The more I thought about it, though, I wondered if my husband's behavior had been more rational than that of the Tennessee Department of Correction, which does not allow conjugal visits. This rule hurts not only the incarcerated but also their partners on the outside. Many a lonely night separated from imprisoned loved ones has produced sex-starved affairs, bitter divorces, and a slew of court-ordered DNA tests to prove paternity.

I am guilty of such an affair. At first, I blamed my husband and his MIA status for what seemed to be my justified infidelity. But I soon realized that I, too, was a victim of a system that shamelessly implements this unnatural form of punishment. The stress and strain of trying to be a good wife all but diminished when fine-ass infatuation walked into my life. I was longing for some company—not necessarily sex but conversation and cuddling. The grip of a strong, manly hand around my waist on a Monday, Tuesday, Wednesday, Thursday, and Friday night was much more enticing and soothing than a tight hug and quick passionate kisses at the beginning and end of a five-hour visit on a Saturday or Sunday.

After so many years behind bars, my husband seemed to be just a non-supportive homey with whom I shared a last name. I was so mad at him for leaving me over and over again. But then I realized that God had given us the freedom to choose our way and that my resentment toward my husband meant that I wasn't allowing him his God-given free will to sleep in the bed that he'd made. He had not been forced to sell narcotics; he chose to sell narcotics. He had chosen to separate from his rib and his seed.

So, unwarranted resentment eventually led to a valuable realization.

My husband and I are now great friends. He has even forgiven me for my indiscretion, which I certainly regret. But while many, many prison relationships and marriages have the unrelenting strength and a commitment backed by faith to survive, the trauma that our marriage suffered through those years of separation caused irreparable damage to our future together. We've decided that parting ways will salvage our friendship. We are going through an amicable divorce.

The twelve years I spent as the Mrs. were rough, but they contained memories I would not trade for anything. I still believe that had jail and prison not separated my husband from his rib, we would still be as one. But jail and prison intruded one too many times.

159705. Uno-cinco-nueve-siete-cero-cinco. 507951. I can recite that number backward, forward, upside down, inside out, or while chewing gum and patting my head.

My name is Vickie Nelson and I am the soon to be ex-wife of TDOC inmate number 159705.

Darrin Goldberg

A Dog Named Regret

S OME SAY THAT A DOG IS A MAN'S BEST FRIEND, but I have to tell you that I wholeheartedly disagree, at least when it comes to a particular dog that I have come to know all too intimately over the past several years. He's not an ordinary dog—not by any stretch of the imagination—but some of his most prevalent behavior patterns and characteristics are so dog-like that I can only equate him with man's closest four-legged friend. And therein lies the great danger because, unlike an ordinary dog who faithfully serves his master, this dog somehow always managed to have his master faithfully serve him.

I met this particular dog early Friday morning, August 9, 1996. The moon shone brightly in a cloudless sky, and chirping birds gave life to the stillness that occurs right before dawn. And there I was at 4:30 in the morning, running full speed away from a crime scene, with blood-stained clothes and a pocket full of the proceeds.

I had just finished a long night of hanging out and partying with a friend who would become my co-defendant, and we were on our way back to Brooklyn. I had to fill up the gas tank, so I stopped at an all-night gas station, which had a small convenience store annexed to it. As we approached the mart, we could see that there was only one person inside. My friend looked at me; I looked at him. We instantly knew what the other was thinking: This is going to be easy. Criminal minds think alike, and since we had tricked away our fair share of money that night, the opportunity to quickly get it all back was too good to pass up.

He pulled out his gun, and we both ran inside the store under the cover of darkness. As we burst inside, the store attendant saw us and came alive with fear. Before he could manage to do anything, however, we were on top of him. This wasn't the first time we had spontaneously done something like this. We knew exactly what to say and how to act to elicit the desired result: We cocked the gun's hammer, pointed it at the attendant, pushed him around a bit, and accompanied it all with threats of death.

We didn't really have any intentions of hurting him, or so I thought. I know I didn't, and I assumed my friend didn't either because we had never hurt anybody before. We would simply run into the establishment, wave the gun, make a few threats, get the money, and take off. Things didn't work out so smoothly this time.

After the attendant emptied his pockets and opened the cash register, he sank into the background as we greedily gorged ourselves on the proceeds. Another job well done, we thought. Then, I instinctively turned around to see where the attendant was, and I could hardly believe my eyes. With two armed thugs in his presence, he had the nerve to pick up the phone and dial 911. That was just totally unacceptable. I turned to my friend, who had been oblivious as he plundered the place, and said, "Yo, he's calling the cops."

My friend turned around and saw the attendant on the phone, and it was as if something snapped inside of him. It was probably because he had been drinking heavily and continuously from the previous evening and was thoroughly intoxicated. Whatever it was, without uttering even a word, he lifted the gun and began striking the attendant in the head. Blood splattered everywhere, and the attendant slumped to the floor.

I couldn't believe what had just happened, but it was real enough. The attendant was still conscious, squirming around on the floor with blood pouring from his head. My initial, brazen confidence quickly turned to fear—in an instant, the situation had become gravely serious. I looked again at my friend; he looked at me, and we knew that it was time to leave now. But before we left he told me to grab some tape and bind the attendant so that he couldn't get up to call the police or read my license plate. In a state of panic, and without thinking, I grabbed the tape with my bare hands and wrapped it around the attendant's ankles, wrists, and eyes. We then rushed headlong out the door into darkness.

It was at that moment when I met my dog, Regret. I was running back to my car, trying to get away, when I heard what sounded like footsteps quickly approaching behind me.

"What was I thinking about?" flashed through my mind. "How could I have done something like that?" I turned around to see what the noise was, and there he was chasing after me. At first I thought he was a guard dog wanting to attack me, but this was not the case. An attack dog growls and flashes its teeth as it aggressively pursues you, but this dog did no such thing. In fact, he seemed mild-tempered and harmless, even though he was barking. Of course, the last thing I needed was a barking dog trailing me. I had to get him to stop, one way or another.

"Can't you see I'm trying to get away with a crime?" I yelled at him. "You're distracting me and bringing me unwanted attention with all that noise. Just get away from me; I don't have time to deal with you right now."

But he didn't go away. He kept barking and staring at me with his deep, penetrating eyes, as if he craved my attention. The weird thing was that the more I looked at him, the more I felt drawn to him and compelled to take him with me. Plus, I didn't want him barking and chasing us. So I put him in the car, and the three of us drove away, beginning our long journey together.

The first stage of that journey took us to the county jail. I managed to get away that night and made it back to Brooklyn, but my escape was short-lived. My friend, who hadn't bothered to cover his face, was captured on a surveillance video. And my fingerprints were found on the duct tape I used to tie up the attendant.

For my part in the crime, I was charged with first- and second-degree robbery, weapons possession, and assault. My lawyer told me that I was looking at ten years in prison if convicted after a trial, or I could accept a plea offer of seven years. Some choice that is, I thought, so I decided that I might as well go to trial.

I was completely stressed out and, to tell the truth, my dog wasn't much help to me then. Although he was right by my side, his very presence was a source of great anxiety. Every single morning he would jump in the bed with me, lick my face, and startle me out of my sleep. "What are we doing here?" he would routinely bark to me. "How could you be so stupid?"

With that grand introduction to each new day, I would get out of bed and go over to the sink to wash up. Looking in the mirror, I would see him over my shoulder and hear him proclaim, "Look at you now, you loser." So many times I wanted to kick him out, but I just couldn't bring myself to do it. Why? Because I was lonely, and he was the only real companion I had in that empty cell. He spent time with me when others were starting to stray away because of my inevitable and rapidly approaching conviction. I felt as if I owed him some measure of loyalty.

As the days passed by, however, my increased sheepishness around him only served to embolden him, and he became more vocal than ever. This was especially true on the days I had to go to court to face the jury. He knew how much I hated the routine: getting up before dawn so that I could sit in a holding pen on a hard metal bench for three or more hours; being stripped of all my clothing and being told to bend over and spread my buttocks in front of another man; getting shackled around my wrists, waist, and feet, and then to another person for the duration of the long bus ride to court; then sitting hungry in another holding pen in the court building until I returned to the jail at 4:00 or 5:00 p.m., just to be strip-searched again.

Nevertheless, my dog would still antagonize me each time I went through the process.

"You thought you were a real man running into that convenience store, didn't you? Now, how much of a man do you feel like, standing naked and spreading your buttocks for another man? Why didn't you just go home that night like you planned on doing? Or, if you were going to commit a crime, why didn't you wear gloves? How could you be so stupid?" His barking was like fingernails scraping against a chalkboard, annoying me and provoking me, with the end result of making me angry—with everybody.

I was angry with myself principally because I got caught. I was angry with my co-defendant for going overboard in the store, and then telling the judge I was involved when he accepted his plea offer. I was angry with my family and so-called friends who were not as supportive as I felt they should have been. I was angry with the store attendant, the victim, because he didn't just give us the money and fall back as everybody else had done, and because he testified against me. And I was angry with my lawyer because I was still in jail and not home with my newborn son, where I belonged.

That anger increased exponentially when I was convicted by a jury and subsequently sentenced to a sixteen-year term of imprisonment. I was devastated, especially since my co-defendant received a fifteen-year sentence, and my lawyer had said that I would only receive ten years if I were convicted after a trial. How would I manage to get through all that time? How would my family cope without me? How would my son flourish without his father? With all the panic, hurt, and frustration I was experiencing at that time, I needed a friend who would comfort me and encourage me so that I could pull through. But there was no one, except for my dog, who eagerly awaited my return to the empty cell so that he could let me have it.

"We're not going home now, are we?" he asked sarcastically. "In fact, we're not going home for a long time, right? You always screw everything up. Look at all the people you hurt and disappointed. I mean, what kind of father are you, leaving your son all alone? Now you won't see his first steps, his first teeth, his first birthday, his first day of school, and his first Little League game. What if something happens to him because you aren't there to protect him? How could you do that to him when you had a father who was always there for you? How could you be so stupid?"

We then moved on to the second stage of our journey together, a New York State maximum-security penitentiary. That's when the dynamics of our relationship changed dramatically. Previously, I had felt in control, determining when I would summon him to spend time with me, what we would talk about, and when we would part. Once I got upstate, however, he became the master, dominating me and dictating my every move with his insatiable appetite for attention. Before long, it was as if his presence in my life paralyzed me and thwarted my attempts to move forward and to grow.

Every single day it was the same thing, with him reminding me of all that I had lost during my time in prison. "Remember all the beautiful women that you loved? If you had even committed yourself to one of them, you would have been so happy right now. Remember all the good jobs you had? If you would have just kept working hard, you would have been so well off right now, instead of being forced to work for sixteen cents an hour. Remember how close you were to your father and mother? If you would have continued to do the right things in life, you could have given them the honor and joy they deserve in return for all the hard work and sacrifices they undertook to raise you. Remember all the goals and aspirations you had, which certainly could have been achieved? Now they are void, and all you have to show for your life's work is wasted years in prison. How could you be so stupid?"

What's more, as if the drama of a serious conviction and a long sentence were not enough, I experienced some of the more commonplace misfortunes found in prison.

My girlfriend, the mother of my son, decided that she couldn't deal with this situation, so she moved on with her life. At first I was mad at her, but then my dog reminded me how badly I used to treat her when I was running around town with other women while she was craving my love and affection. So, I guess I can't blame her, but it sure would have been nice to see or hear from my son in the last six years.

My oldest brother died at only thirty-six years old. It was difficult mourning for him because I was locked in a double-bunked cell when it happened, and it's just not proper prison etiquette to cry in a cramped-up cell with another convict present. Plus, the prison wouldn't let me attend his funeral. My mother's bills were so backed up that she couldn't take the block off her phone so that I could call collect and we could speak. The pain was indescribable, but my dog was there to remind me that I should feel lucky—most convicts doing a long stretch of time lose several close loved ones, and I only lost one. I guess he was right. I just wish I could have told my brother that I loved him, since I can't remember ever doing that and now will never have the opportunity.

The more time I spend with my dog Regret, the more I realize how much I rely on him, and how much deference I give to his opinions. Most times that translates into my feeling down in the dumps and depressed because he is merciless in his approach.

But then there are times when his blunt remarks make me feel pretty good about myself. The way I see it, if he wasn't around me saying those things, then that would indicate that I am a bad person, and that I have no problems with my past deeds. Conversely, as long as he is in my life and I continue to accept his abuse, then that is a clear and indisputable indication that I have changed for the better, and that I detest my past deeds. That is why I continue to be a glutton for punishment, and willingly acquiesce to his mostly demeaning and otherwise intolerable presence.

But now that we have entered the third, and final, stage of our journey together, I intuitively sense that things must change. I have been transferred to a medium-security prison, which means that I will be going home soon. I just don't think I can take him with me, despite the fact that we have grown attached to each other. For one, he's just far too possessive. I mean, this dog wants my attention all the time; he wants me to listen to him and pet him all day, every day. Even on those rare occasions when I leave him behind so that I can spend time with someone else, he always manages to track my scent and show up at my side. And the worst part about it is that all he wants to do is talk about the past, as if he has no visions or positive ambitions and only enjoys reminiscing.

If that's not enough, this dog is also far too expensive for me, and I simply can't afford him anymore. I know I will not be able to feed his insatiable appetite every single day. If I am burdened with that obligation I will be just as I am in here, not being able to do anything else whenever he's around, which is constantly. That can no longer be an option, inasmuch as I am beginning to once again feel hopeful and optimistic about my future and myself. I have so many things that I would like to do.

Now, that doesn't mean I will be able to simply erase all traces of him from my life, or that I'm even interested in doing so. The truth is, my dog Regret has had a significant impact on my life and has taught me so many valuable lessons that I need to take with me. He has taught me that I cannot take anything for granted, and that I should cherish all the good that I have in my life, including those people who had no obligation to support me during this time but did so anyway. He taught me that every action has a consequence and, more important, that once you do something, you can *never* take it back, no matter how much you want to. And he has taught me to be consistently conscious of the fact that every decision I make has the potential to positively or adversely affect scores of other people. So, despite the fact that I really don't like him and regret spending so much time with him when I could've been engaged in more productive and progressive endeavors, I appreciate the fact that he has served his purpose in my life.

Nevertheless, I find myself longing for the moment when I can leave prison and leave him behind. I even have a plan on how to get rid of him. Now, you might find it cruel—and, of course, I would never do this to him if he were an ordinary dog—but my mind is already made up. On the day that I finally walk out these prison doors after thirteen years, when he comes running and wagging his tail, excited about us entering the next stage together, he is in for a terrible surprise.

I am going to look him straight in the eyes, tell him to turn around, and then kick him square in the behind. I can't wait to hear him whining and whimpering as he scampers away from me and I turn to walk out the door alone, never to see his ugly face again.

Ah, how great it will be to know that I am finally free of the past, free of the errors I made, and free to focus and work on creating a respectable and successful future. And, herein lies probably the greatest lesson my dog Regret has taught me:

Only when I make positive changes within myself to ensure that I will be a good person in the future, forgive myself for past deeds I committed but can no longer change, and get rid of the debilitating Regret, can I truly say that I am free. As I prepare to go home, I am happy to say that I am.

Corey John Richardson

How Some Men Find Love

W E DON'T ALWAYS DO THE RIGHT THINGS. I rarely did. A few years ago, I was facing a lot of prison time for a rather atypical white-collar crime. My co-defendant had just taken a deal in the middle of our joint trial. For those of you not familiar with the system, this ensured that I would be the one to go away for quite awhile.

I was paralyzed with fear. Surely, I would be a target in prison, and not just because of my rather obvious middle-class demeanor or my high-profile case. I am gay. Not in an overt way. I never steeped myself in the gay culture. I am just gay. As I waited for that day when I would be transported to a concrete world behind a razor-wire fence, the prison violence documentaries shown on cable were foremost in my mind—not my favorite Jeff Stryker videos from college, when he made all his sexual conquests in the local county lock-up.

Yet, oddly enough, I developed a fantasy of meeting someone in prison. This was certainly not some gang-bang, rape-fest fantasy, but about meeting some strong young soul who needed love just as much as I did. The world had thrown me away. In prison, the Land of the Throw-Aways, there's much hunger for love (and food and money and freedom), and it mutates into behaviors difficult to explain.

I have heard that the Roman armies, the Spartans, and other cultures of the ancient world embraced homosexuality. When you lock men up for decades at a time, it is quite easy to figure out why it becomes natural for some to seek the arms of another man. There are just men, men, and more men, year after long year. It was just as natural for the ancients, with their long campaigns to conquer distant lands. Perfectly straight men become situationally gay, or at least for a time. Homosexual acts in prison facilitate sexual release and sometimes fill the need for love.

After I got settled in my cell, I walked around the prison. I tried to look natural, but surely my eyes were as big as half dollars. My nerves were shredded. It did not take long to see a few "sissies," a few "punks," and a few "boys" (common prison nomenclature), all walking with their respective "friends." Gay men were in quite larger numbers than I had expected in prison. How could this be? Had drinking, drugs, or just plain stupidity brought them to prison like it had me? It would seem so.

Gay men in prison are an unusual bunch. Some are under-cover and some are proud, tough queens. Some are just rather average. Many gay men in prison distinctly assume female affectations. They aren't transgendered, though prison has plenty of transgendered men, too. To some gay men, female attributes are bait, and many straight convicts are more open to sex with another man when they perceive a female illusion orchestrated with shaven legs and plucked eyebrows.

I was lonely, but that just wasn't me.

After a few weeks it was overwhelmingly clear to me that prison—at least in this state—was a 24/7 meat market. This is what had terrified me? And, while several hundred men were trying to figure out if I was merely a "fish," easily tricked or perchance gay, I had already decided to plant myself in the path of the biggest, most beautiful young buck this world has ever known. Eventually, he sat down beside me and said hello.

As a gay man, I had often felt, underneath the surface, rejected and alone, but now I felt utterly destroyed. I hoped to find some companionship. I hoped he would be the one. It was more than I could have ever dreamed possible. It was instant. He loved my knowledge, my worldview, and our multitude of differences.

He dragged me to the weight pile, took me to chow hall, and even tried to teach me basketball. We shared meals in the dorm, watched movies on the weekend and, well...we didn't just screw. This man made love to me as no one else ever had. It was wonderful each and every time. This was a man so straight that I was terrified to even kiss him that first time. This straight man completely, unreservedly, met every need that I had sexually and otherwise. I also found several needs that I had not known even existed. No man that I had ever known was stronger, more tender and sensitive.

Then he was gone. We shared about a year together before he made parole. As much as I thought I had appreciated him, it was only a fraction of what he deserved. He held me in his arms as I cried real honest-to-goodness tears. This man loved me as I was. He never asked for more from me than my time and love.

I still do the same workouts. Still cook the same meals. Still run the same track. I still smile when I think about his beautiful face laughing in the summer sun as we walked together across the prison yard.

Prison is still a 24/7 meat market, but I never found love again. I still see men—gay and straight—finding comfort in each other's arms. But as I edge closer toward release, being pursued has lost its luster. When my love left, I began to discover more of myself.

One thing is certain: I grew into the man I always wanted to be in prison, but not because of it—in spite of it.

Don't think that the corrections administration accepts gays, or that prison is safe. Neither is true. A fight in prison may cost you fifteen days in segregation, but get caught in the arms of another man and you will spend ninety days in "the hole" and you will get six months added to your sentence due to loss of good time.

Purchasing condoms on the black market is nearly impossible and the medical departments are loathe to offer expensive HIV testing. Think of this: "Barely Legal" porn magazines showing underage girls are permissible, but a gay political or literary magazine is considered contraband and, therefore, not permitted into the institution. Those magazines allegedly "promote homosexuality." But in reality, serving ten, twenty, and thirty years or longer—not a magazine—promotes homosexual acts.

Straight men in prison do not see their partners inside as particularly male. These couples still fight like those in the free world. Some are even abusive. Some cheat. Many scam lonely gay men through pen pal services. Sometimes gays need to fight like everyone else. Everyone, gay or straight, misses their families and their freedom. It is still prison.

When my friend left, he went to live with his parents, who were raising his twin sons. In his enthusiasm over us, he told his mother the whole truth. But, I wonder if I was merely part of his prison experience, after all. We often joked, "What happens in prison stays in prison." Maybe when he shed his prison attire, he shed me, too, but I hope not completely.

I pray that part of what we were lingers still. He said before he left that I had changed him forever. I felt the same, and still do. After having been truly loved for the first time in my life, I found that I was finally proud of myself without reservations. I was glad to have been born gay. Maybe now I could find real love once again upon my release, but this time with another gay man. Imagine that!

Mother Teresa once said that we humans are angels with only one wing and that we need each other to fly. He helped me get from that place of loss and confusion to the sure footing of where I am today. I hardly knew that it was happening. What an odd place for it all to have occurred.

Frank Reid

A Love Against All Odds

> *"Love is contraband in Hell,*
> *cause love is a acid that eats away bars."*
> —*Assata Shakur*

I T'S BEEN EXACTLY THREE YEARS since I got her first letter. It wasn't very long, but I could tell from the fanciful writing that much care had been taken to compose it.

Her name is Kate P., and she introduced herself as a friend of a friend. She had been given a manuscript that another prisoner and I had written together, and she wanted to know if I would submit a brief autobiography to accompany it. She was preparing the final manuscript for a potentially interested publisher and thought the book would be more appealing if we included more personal detail in what was overwhelmingly a political dialogue. Her bubbly personality invigorated the letters on the page like a waltz, and she ended the missive with a graceful "No Reservations."

I wondered, who was this friend of a friend, who was interested in helping me to gain a voice, a literary platform from which to express my views and beliefs? I wrote the short autobiography and mailed it to Kate. I was eager to get the publishing process going, to offer up my intellectual contribution to the social change to which I'd committed myself.

As the weeks passed, Kate and I became acquainted through letters, which were lively and thoughtful. Our correspondence brightened my gloomy and uneventful existence in a prison in the secluded mountains of southwest Virginia.

Kate and I discovered that we are both committed to societal change. We discovered, too, that we are from different racial, cultural, and socioeconomic backgrounds. She is a young white woman; I am a young black man. Undaunted by the differences, we held on to the lifeline of our humanity, sharing intimate details about our lives. In fact, there wasn't one aspect of our lives that remained unexplored.

It was a chilly day in March 2006 when I heard the familiar "beep" from the intercom in my cell. The authoritative voice of a male corrections officer invaded my living quarters. "Reid, you got a visit. Get ready."

I hurried to the sink and washed my hands and face. I took a swig of mouthwash, cleansing my mouth of the insipid taste of prison breakfast. Taking a final glance in the mirror, I convinced myself that I was presentable. I hit the intercom button to notify the C.O. that I was ready to go.

Kate had told me a few weeks earlier that she would be coming that month but offered no precise dates. I rightly guessed that she was my visitor that day, as my family surely would've told me beforehand if they were coming.

Walking to the visiting room with a sense of importance, I was excited to finally meet a person who was inspired by the same ideals as mine. I immediately spotted her at the opposite end, on the left side of the aisle that stretches the length of the visiting room. Even though I'd never seen a picture of her, I knew it was Kate. I strolled toward her, careful not to overstep the red tape on the floors on both sides of my path. She stood up, bearing a cheerful smile as we both leaned across the table and over the metal partition between us to embrace in a warm, welcoming hug.

She smelled of a vanilla fragrance. She exuded a child-like effervescence, combined somehow with a ladylike air of sophistication. She had long, thick, golden brown hair; it was done up in a ponytail and fell to the middle of her upper back. She was pleasing to the eyes.

I couldn't help thinking that she was out of place, perhaps lost. She seemed so innocent. I stared into her grayish-green eyes, searching for clues as to where she got the courage (and compassion) to board a Greyhound bus in New York City and travel over 1,000 miles to meet me.

"Miles and miles apart...lying next to her in my heart."
—*Frank Reid*

From the outset of corresponding, Kate and I had given considerable attention to the dynamics of interracial love relationships, including how our children would be perceived or would question their own identities. Being highly political, I was also concerned about how I could "rationalize" being with a white woman when I subscribe to what is commonly called "identity politics."

When our friendship grew into intimate love, we began to view our relationship through the lens of prison. The three years I've been in a relationship with Kate have entailed a great deal of compromise—not so much with her, as with the prison. No matter how we have decided to relate to one another, the scope of our interaction remains overly determined by the institution of prison.

If a particular desire violates prison rules and policies, we must dismiss it or place it in emotional storage until time and opportunity allow for fulfillment.

That I'm in a super-max prison further compounds the difficulties inherent in our relationship. Visitation rules are stringent, policies governing prisoner correspondence are overly restrictive, and the prison guards are hostile toward interracial relationships.

Kate and I have had to overcome seemingly insurmountable odds, both internal and external, to finally arrive at a place where we now both feel secure in a stable prison relationship.

Her friends launched the first of the external "assaults" on us. After breaking the news of our relationship to them, Kate was repeatedly met with ridicule and hysteria for being involved with a prisoner. They were skeptical of my character and intentions and the sincerity of my love for Kate. A few hurled long-range insults at me. One friend abruptly cut off all contact with Kate because of her involvement with me.

As a result, Kate vowed to keep our relationship to herself in order to avoid further emotional turmoil and criticism. I was ambivalent about her reaction, and that of her friends. While I can't defend myself from character assassinations at the hands of her friends, I expected Kate, as my significant other, to defend me and not retreat from the commitments we'd made to each other by keeping our relationship hidden like some shameful secret. While I understood her friends' concerns for her well-being, I did not appreciate that they had prejudged me in a stereotypical way without knowing me or attempting to know me. I also did not appreciate how unsupportive they were of Kate's decision to love me for who I am.

On the other hand, I had to come to grips with the fact that by being in a prison relationship, Kate and I are challenging society's conceptions of a "normal" relationship. It was insensitive and unfair of me to shoulder Kate with the tremendous burden of proving to the world that our love is perfectly normal.

Internally, Kate and I were struggling over the definition and practical workings of our relationship. Early on, Kate proposed that we be in an "open relationship." I rejected this idea. I understood her suggestion as an attempt to practically deal with the reality of physical separation in prison relationships. But I felt that being intimate with other people would not be conducive to a healthy relationship between Kate and me. I would have preferred that we remain friends than be a party to what, in my opinion, is a mockery of a serious, committed relationship. Yet, Kate shuddered at my suggestion that we simply be "friends."

The institution of prison, and how it intrudes on our relationship, remained a source of confusion, frustration, bitter disagreement, and even a few break-ups. Our particular prison relationship is marked by physical separation existing side by side with intense emotional attachment. Because so much of our lives cannot be observed by the other, our relationship calls for a lot of honesty and trust.

Essentially, our problem is trying to navigate the reality of living apart as a couple, while being careful not to place demands that could possibly destroy us as a couple. Neither of us wants to lose the other. Under these circumstances, it's been a challenge negotiating mutually acceptable compromise.

Communicating through letters and phone calls on a consistent basis helps us cope. Every letter, picture, phone call, birthday card, poem, visit, anniversary, special day, hour, minute, "I love you," is vital to maintaining our connectedness. Having a support network of friends who are also in prison relationships, or are at least receptive to us, has had a profoundly positive influence on us. Those friends have helped Kate, and by extension me, weather the alienation we've experienced in our relationship.

"I got your back, I'm by your side, and that's for life...even though we argue sometimes."
—*Stic.Man and Young Noble*

Somehow, through every period of heartache and pain, Kate and I managed to emerge from the destructive flames of calamity, hand in hand, practically unscathed. But neither of us foresaw the magnitude of the storm clouds gathering in early 2007.

By late 2006, Kate had been visiting me quite regularly, traveling down to Virginia from New York. I relished our visits. However, as an interracial couple, we remained at the epicenter of the prison guards' attention and scrutiny. Our relationship is taboo at a prison located in a predominantly white region of Virginia with rigid racial boundaries. The guards balked at our open displays of affection. They were disturbed to see a black man and white woman in a passion-ate embrace, our tongues caressing the warm, wet surfaces of each other's mouths.

On several occasions I had been reprimanded for having made 'inappropriate' contact with Kate. It was plain to see that, in the guards' view, my whole relationship with Kate was inappropriate. We knew the guards had it in for us and were just waiting for the perfect opportunity to drive a permanent wedge between us.

That opportunity came on a holiday weekend in January 2007. Kate was visiting me for four consecutive days. The first three days went exceptionally well. On the fourth day, after we'd been in the visiting room for about ten minutes, a mob of prison guards encircled us. A ranking guard asked to speak with Kate. With a smug expression on his face, he told her that she must immediately leave the prison premises—her visits had been suspended. I sulked in my chair. Kate turned around to face me in disbelief, confused, and on the verge of crying. I stood and hugged her as tightly as I could, not sure when or if I would see her again. While we embraced, I calmly said to her, "I need you to stay strong, baby; we gon' get through this."

Watching Kate leave the visiting room, I was angry. But I stoically walked back to my cell, saying nothing to the three guards escorting me.

We found out that Kate's visits had been suspended statewide because she had a verbal confrontation with a prison guard while trying to visit a mutual friend at nearby Red Onion Prison. She was denied entry there without prior notification. As a consequence, the warden at Red Onion permanently suspended Kate's visits. It was a racially and politically motivated act. The fact that Kate and I were in an interracial relationship only heightened the prison officials' seething rage.

The flames of rage were fanned in other ways, too. As I said, both Kate and I are committed to changing society. Our mutual friend in prison and I have been active in bringing to light the abuse and mistreatment of prisoners in southwest Virginia. The fact that Kate was an instrumental link to the outside world—providing legal, financial, and moral support—made her a worthy target of retaliation for prison officials.

I didn't see Kate again for six months, not until July 2007. She was with our friend Becky and had been granted informal permission to see me by the warden. It was the last time I'd see her that year.

Through an extraordinary show of teamwork, perseverance, and unified strength, Kate and I endured that stressful and discouraging time when we couldn't see each other. With Kate on the outside calling and writing prison officials in the upper echelons of the Virginia Department of Corrections, and me on the inside utilizing the prison grievance system, we succeeded in getting her visitation privileges reinstated. It was a defining moment in our relationship.

On March 28, 2008, I received official notification in the mail that Kate was permitted to see me. I was ecstatic. The next morning I rushed to the phone to tell her the wonderful news. Surprisingly, Becky answered. She told me that Kate was on her way to visit me at that moment. Kate had already received notice earlier in the week that her visits had been reinstated. The only downside was that we had to undergo a ninety-day "probationary" period of no-contact visits.

That next afternoon, I joyfully looked at Kate. Even through the thick glass that separated us, I could feel the depth of our devotion to each other.

Randy Peters

The Visit

RANDY PACES HIS SMALL CELL. Its few furnishings cramp the white enclosure. Two bunks stacked on the left wall are covered with thin, hard mattresses. One tiny steel table is bolted to the right wall, with a green plastic chair slid partially under it. In a corner by the door sits a stainless steel toilet-sink combo. The polished metal mirror over it catches distorted reflections as he paces by. Even at 5'6", he needs only four short strides to get to the blue, double-steel door. He opens it and peers through its narrow rectangle of Plexiglas that serves as a window. He checks the clock on the dayroom wall for the third time in as many minutes.

"She should be here by now," he mutters. He spins on his heels and pulls the door shut behind him.

Randy strides to the recessed window overlooking the parking lot. He bounces his head off the heavy metal screen while scanning the blacktop.

"I wish I knew what she drives now."

Sunlight flashes off a moving windshield; his heart leaps. "Is that her?" The chain link fence breaks up his view of an old Ford pulling in. Disappointment slaps him. "Nope, not her. She wouldn't drive a Ford on a bet."

He resumes pacing, with his stomach twisting and gurgling. Meager food portions and anxiety are a bad mixture. He winces as nausea threatens to overtake him. A low growl rumbles in his throat; he rides the wave of sickness until it calms. The battle leaves him breathless. While he stands panting, hands on his knees, the guard calls his name.

"Peters, let's go; you got a visit."

Randy straightens and struggles for composure. He strolls to the sally port door beside the officer and waits to be let out. The correctional officer ignores him, just for fun. Randy bites his tongue; he's been through this before. Any comment on his part will bring a confrontation. Inmates always lose confrontations with C.O.s, right, wrong, or otherwise. The guard finally realizes he can't goad Randy into a fight and pushes a button on his console. The lock pops; Randy steps through, closes the door, and waits for the second to open. Once that obstacle is cleared, another door stands at the exit. He pushes a call button mounted on the wall and waits, tapping his foot and chewing on his lip. His actions must be measured and nonaggressive. A camera on the ceiling behind him feeds a screen in main control; a speaker in the call box picks up every word. Any word or movement considered improper by either of the two guards in main control will result in Randy being locked in his cell, missing precious visit time.

This door pops and he walks into the yard—a glob of grass dropped in the middle of four concrete buildings and peppered with three round picnic tables anchored by buried, concrete tubes. Forgotten balls are scattered across the vacant lot. A sense of loneliness and despair hangs in the air.

At the end of his fifty-yard hike is another sally port guarding the main building. Randy gnaws on his lip while he waits to get in. Two adjacent doors open simultaneously and he enters the hall. A guard waits at the far end. A vicious pat-down leaves him limping toward the visiting room. He looks through the large entrance window and his heart soars. Donna smiles and waves.

Her long, thick, auburn hair frames her face in a perfect complement to her blue eyes. She let it grow to the middle of her back because Randy loves it that way. The very sight of her melts away the pain of prison. He bounces on his toes, impatient for her embrace. His heart rate triples when the door opens. He rushes to her open arms.

They lean over one of several octagonal tables lined in a half circle to separate them. A C.O. jumps up from his post next to the visitors' entry and runs to stop them. Noise from the children's play area makes him barely audible.

"Hey, hey, none of that. There's no more contact during visits."

Randy's voice holds a hint of anger. "Why? I didn't do anything wrong."

"New policy. Last week we caught a grandmother in a wheelchair trying to smuggle in drugs."

"What's that got to do with me?"

"Like I said, no more contact."

"So, because some asshole I don't even know tries to get drugs, I gotta suffer?"

" 'Fraid so."

Randy's eyes smolder and a growl builds in his chest.

Donna's nervous response douses his fire. "It's okay, honey, let's just visit. We don't get much time together. I don't want to lose any."

Randy pulls out the black and chrome chair. "You're right, baby, let's visit."

The guard returns to his desk; Randy's glare burns holes in his back.

Donna chances a brush across her husband's hand. "How you been, honey?"

"Miserable. You?"

"Depressed, lonely, broke, sad, angry. Did I mention lonely? I've come to terms with the fact that you can't come home, but I wish you were closer. Seeing you once every six weeks sucks."

"Yes, it does. The Department of Corrections preaches they want us to stay in contact with our families, then they drag us as far away as possible."

"I'm not sure how I'm going to handle another year of this."

"I know it's hard on you, babe; I don't like it either. I can't sleep. I toss and turn from missing you. I try to stay positive, but it's hard."

Randy can see the depths of loneliness in her eyes. It drives a corkscrew of pain and guilt into his heart. "Have you tried to get out and see friends?"

"I did go up to Eddie and Lisa's."

"I really wish you wouldn't go up there."

"You just said you wanted me to go see friends. I don't have that many, you know."

"I do know. I just wish you'd stay away from Eddie. I know how he is. He'll use your loneliness to try to get in your pants."

"Thanks for the vote of confidence."

"I don't mean to insult you, honey. The loneliness really gnaws at me, all the time, and I know you hate to be alone even more than I do. Eddie's a fucking predator; he'll jump on that in a heartbeat."

"So, I should just stay home and not talk to anybody?"

"I'm not saying that. I just wish you'd find some new friends is all."

"I can't find new friends. I'm no good with people. I don't trust them."

Randy's head drops to his chest; he draws in a long, slow breath. "I love you, baby. I love you with all my heart. I want you to be happy, but I worry every day about losing you."

"You're not gonna lose me, honey."

"I try to believe that, and I know you mean it, but I also know that everybody has a limit, a breaking point. I'm scared to death you're gonna find yours before I get out."

Donna's soft blue eyes hold his in a comforting embrace. "I'm not gonna find my breaking point. I'm too tough for that."

Randy forces a smile. "Will you at least do one thing for me?"

"Anything."

"Don't hang around Eddie unless Lisa's right there and, for God's sake, don't let him get you to drinkin'."

"That's two things, honey."

"I'm serious, babe. This shit scares the hell outta me. You're the only reason I got for livin'. "

"Okay, honey, I'll do what you ask."

"Thank you."

The guard's bellow echoes across the room. "Time's up; visit's over; everybody out. C'mon, let's go."

Donna slumps under the weight of the words. "These things never last long enough," she says, sighing and putting on a brave face. "Are you gonna call me tomorrow?"

"Definitely."

"Good. I can't wait. I love you, honey."

"I love you, too, baby. I love you with all my heart. Try to remember that when things get tough."

"I will."

The guard lands a disgusted look on Randy. "Peters, if you don't wanna lose your visiting privileges, you'll quit yakking, *right now*."

Donna, getting up, sees the rage in Randy's eyes. "It's okay, honey. I'll talk to you tomorrow; try to stay calm 'til then."

"I'll try. Bye, baby. I love you."

"I love you too, honey. Bye."

Randy's heart withers as he watches Donna walk away. The emptiness is already rising inside him.

She turns. He gives her one last wink and wave. She smiles, blowing him a kiss on her way out the door. Then the slamming door chops off his happiness like a guillotine.

Randy sighs and swallows his tears.

He rises and gets in line for his least favorite part of prison, the strip search. It's the most humiliating thing he's ever been through. After hundreds of them, he's still not used to it. The sense of violation is akin to being raped, especially when you're homophobic. He grits his teeth while trying to clear his mind. Pictures of Donna getting drunk and succumbing to her loneliness torture his thoughts. When he pushes those away, they are replaced by his most prominent waking nightmare—Donna telling him she's had enough, that she can't take the stress anymore. The stress of facing a strip search and what he may face in the future is overwhelming. Tightness in his chest makes him wonder if he's going to have a heart attack.

Randy steps into the dreaded room. He struggles to imagine himself walking in the woods, in hopes the distraction will take him away from the degradation he's about to endure.

Running through the mechanical motions of the strip search, the C.O.'s directions are barely heard. "Run your hands through your hair. Lift your arms, now your feet. Raise your scrotum, turn around, bend over and spread 'em. Alright, you're good."

Randy straightens and tries to control his erratic breathing. He reaches to retrieve his clothes from the officer. He is stunned to the point of vomiting when the guard smiles and winks at him. Randy wrestles with an urge to fight. He dresses as fast as possible then scurries out the door. He knows striking an officer will add at least two years to his sentence, a long two years he can't afford. He is so freaked by the guard's blatant advance, he breaks into cold chills. He walks down the hall shivering and fighting an overwhelming queasiness. His mind blacks out in self-defense.

The next thing he knows, he's back in his cell, lying on his bunk. His mind is tortured with worry over Donna. There's nothing he can do, no way he can change things. The crushing sense of hopelessness steals his breath. All he can do is sit and wonder how long he'll have to wait before he gets another visit.

Safiya E. Bandele

The Illness

THE ROOM REEKS OF DEATH. The smell pours from the various fluids flowing to and from his body via the intersecting tubes. The varied redness of his blood competes with the urine yellowness of another fluid—all in the midst of a sometimes clear, sometimes mucusy liquid also meandering through the tubes. The muted tones of the light behind his bed cast a yellow pall over everything, similar to the subdued tones of floor lamps at the head of a casket in a funeral parlor.

Located in the hospital's intensive care unit, the two-patient room is also prison.

When I walk in, he's on his side watching a small television. The sheet covering his body highlights his gauntness. The sharp, bony part of his hip thrusts upward. Immediately, I'm reminded of his mother, Emma Lee. She died a painful death after a slow deterioration over several years. She spent her final days lying in bed curled in the fetal position and finally died a few weeks after he graduated from high school. That's who he looks like lying there in that room. Curled in the fetal position just like his mama. Is he just wasting away, too?

It was said that Emma Lee got sick and died a slow death because she had been messing with somebody's husband and somebody had "worked roots" on her. They took her to the "root doctor" in the Alabama countryside. Her death certificate lists the cause of death as "natural causes." She was forty-seven years old, had borne eleven children, and had never married.

One of her sons, this one named Kenyatta, was now near death thirty years later—December 1994—in St. Agnes Hospital in upstate New York. He was being kept in the hospital's prison ward, which housed inmates of New York State's Fishkill Prison. A prison nurse had called me—"the person to notify," according to Kenyatta's records—to tell me that he had been admitted to St. Agnes on December 21. But because only immediate family members were allowed to visit in the prison ward, I had to get special permission from the Fishkill warden to see him.

My own life-long woman's psychic illness of indecision paralleled Kenyatta's physical illness. I've always had the tendency to say one thing and feel the opposite on certain issues—to feel one thing and do the opposite. Getting permission from the warden brought up one of those issues: marriage. For many reasons, we had decided not to marry under his conditions of incarceration. But I had often wanted marriage as a kind of validation of our relationship, and now I thought how much easier it would be if I were his "wife" and could visit without special permission.

I worried that I might have to get a court order to see him. I thought about all the years I had been with him (more or less since 1969) and all the traumas and joys of our journey.

Eventually, the Fishkill prison superintendent granted me permission, and I made the trip to the upstate hospital, travelling on the commuter railroad to White Plains, New York. Despite the fact that he was critically ill in a hospital, I still had to be processed—it was still a prison visit—my identification checked and body searched by a female prison guard before being escorted inside. It was strange to walk the corridors of a hospital that was also a prison.

When I enter his room, two prison guards—one male, one female—position themselves outside the room. The tiny television's flickering light helps illuminate the dimness. The sheets' whiteness contrasts with Kenyatta's blackness, his dreadlocks spread out over the pale pillow. He half-rises when I sweep in and gives me a big smile. Feeling somewhat uneasy, I throw my coat on a chair and walk around the bed to hug him. I take him in my arms, almost lifting his long, frail frame off the bed, kissing his face all over—his eyes, mouth, cheeks, his neck, his ears, under his arms. His underarm! A shock of sexual delight! I love his underarm smell. So I sniff, drink it in like a woman dying of thirst. I don't even mind the rankness resulting from his days of not bathing while we harassed the prison authorities to send a doctor to his cell to examine him.

As we embrace, I am aware of the two prison guards sitting outside the room, staring in alarm and confusion. I can sense them wondering whether they should break up our intimacy. The female guard asks her male partner, "Who is she?" Ignoring their discussion, I sit and watch him. It's only then that I notice his roommate, a fellow prisoner/patient taking in the whole scene.

I study Kenyatta. He looks extremely unnatural, like he's dying. Not from the tube in his penis and hanging bloody bag collecting his urine and other fluids. Not from the tubes and needles in his arms. But from the cumulative result of being denied medical attention during the past months at Fishkill Prison and the compounded effects of twenty years of abuse and exhaustion from prison life. Still, he looks gorgeous. And mad. And crazy.

I'm concerned about his health, but I'm also angry. How dare he die now, before we have a chance to be together. How dare he die now, after I've spent a fortune visiting him and working on his release. Die before we have a chance to make mad love? He better not! I want to FUCK this man! He can't die! I want this man to FUCK me! He better not die! Die before we have a chance to wash dishes and cook together? Die before we have a chance to do all the things most people take for granted—which cannot be ours until he's released from prison?

I watch him. Hold one hand and feel the flesh hanging off his long fingers.

We're both surprised at this turn of events. This illness. This from a man who taught exercise classes in prison. Who was almost legendary for his physical abilities. "I never thought this would happen to me," he says. I watch him.

It's surreal. This is the first time I've even seen him in a bed. It's the first time I've seen his toes (peeking from under the hospital cover) since we met on the IRT Subway in Brooklyn, New York in May 1969, when I noticed his beautiful feet in sandals. I fell in love with those feet. The things I've so often fantasized doing to and with his long toes.

I want to get physical. Close to him. In some kinda way. Any kinda way. So I fix his hair, putting his dreadlocks up in a ponytail. Dinner arrives. I stand to help him. He adds salt, pepper, sugar, and ketchup all over the food—a prison habit to spice up the bland meals. I feed him some soup. He eats little. Making faces and grimacing as he tastes the various items. We talk. I tell him folks are concerned about him. "People are sick when they act like that," he says, "waiting until someone is near death to act." I coax him to eat more, but he's finished.

I suggest he brush his teeth and busy myself getting his toothbrush, toothpaste, and water. Another thrill for me. I've known him for nearly thirty years and this is the first time I've ever seen him brush his teeth. We talk some more, a rambling conversation. He cries. I cry. I don't want to leave.

I worry about his health although we've heard St. Agnes is a good hospital. Still, this is prison. He recounts the story of the catheter. How he hollered when the doctors came near him with that "big-ass tube to stick in my dick." He said even the prison guard was alarmed. I ask him for his medical information, but it's clear his mind isn't functioning properly.

I am scared yet fascinated that this brilliant man's mind is going. Visiting time is up.

The guards stand up to watch me put on my coat and say goodbye. I tell him I'll be back. He smiles and says, "You a good woman, Safiya."

I walk out of his room and down the corridor. At the nurses' station I demand to see Kenyatta's nurse, all my fear and rage at the prison system in my voice. The folks at the nurses' station look alarmed. I probably look as crazy as Kenyatta. His nurse tells me she will talk to both of us.

The guards hesitate, since visiting time is up. But the nurse walks me back to Kenyatta's room. He's sitting up looking at us while she talks. I can see that he doesn't fully understand what's happening. "He has one kidney," she says. (He was born with only one kidney.) It's badly infected. His bladder isn't working. She goes on to describe his medical regimen. He's doing better, according to the nurse. Tests are planned. She speaks professionally and reassuringly.

The next time I visit, the sergeant on duty tells me the nurses' station is off-limits to me.

The first visit was unlike the remaining visits, which I chronicled in a journal. As it became clear that he would live—although "damaged"—the feel of his hospital room began to seem less oppressive. On that first visit I wore my hat and coat inside, but that subsequently was not allowed. Also, my remaining visits took place in a small "visiting room" with a large table and chairs and a guard posted at the door. The guard would escort me there, passing Kenyatta's room along the way. Kenyatta would see me and follow with his catheter and IV pole. We sat at the table, opposite each other.

I usually came for the 5:00 to 7:00 p.m. visit, which included his dinnertime. We both marveled at the fact that he was eating non-prison food for the first time in twenty years, regularly eating things he liked: chicken, milkshakes. I enjoyed watching him eat and he enjoyed watching me watch him.

On several visits he described hearing a sound and "feelin' the movement of the ventilation system grabbin' hold of me, my spirit, 'n carryin' me into this time warp." We wondered if it was related to the sound of the subway that fateful morning—January 1974—when he was arrested on the subway platform.

Kenyatta's hospitalization was an unforgettable period. My issues—as a woman, as his love, as an educator/activist—all played out during "The Illness." Among them was the issue of not being Kenyatta's "immediate family," which resulted in my having to get the warden's approval to see him at St. Agnes. Many folks had asked why we didn't get married so we could at least have "trailer" (conjugal) visits and opportunities to spend time together in an intimate environment. For a long time, we never talked about marriage; we just knew we wanted to be together and believed we always would. At one time I felt he was opposed to it because it required some form of cooperation/participation with his captors—and his stance was one of non-participation. His consistent refusal to appear before the parole board was a form of non-participation. And a counselor had told him that while he had a right to marry, he didn't have a right to trailer visits, which were a form of privilege based on participation in prison programs. I had flirted with the idea of marriage mainly as a validation of self-worth: "Yeah, I can get a husband." But the idea of making love on the prison grounds, bound by rules and regulations, under the prison tower with guns at the ready, was a turnoff. Then my idea about marriage shifted to waiting until Kenyatta came home. But then I realized that it was the same ole need to prove something. So, no.

For the first time since his imprisonment, I saw him in a non-prison environment. And in spite of the hovering guards, it was a positive experience. There were so many "firsts" for us during this time, not only the view of his toes and the non-prison food but the "Visiting Trip" itself. During the years of prison visits, the majority of those early-morning Metro-North riders were Black and Latina women and children. It was just the opposite taking the Metro-North to White Plains with primarily white businessmen.

At St. Agnes, as I waited to visit Kenyatta and observed the regular hospital visitors, I wondered if they knew of the special "Prison Ward" right upstairs. I was always slightly anxious each time I visited, worried about Kenyatta's condition and worried whether the sergeant on duty knew I had special permission to visit.

St. Agnes Hospital has a beautiful chapel whose interior reminds me of St. Alphonsus, the small black Catholic Church of my North Carolina childhood. I was a Catholic girlchild terrified of sex and hell and at the same time thrilled by the idea of both. The Virgin/Whore. That dangerousness, that duality, imprisoned me as a child—and imprisons me to this day.

—Adapted from a story originally published in the online magazine In The Fray, *March 2002.*

Patrick Stephens

The Ugly Butterfly

"**H**I, DAD. HAPPY BIRTHDAY!"

I could still hear my seven-year-old son's voice in my head as I walked up the stairs to my cell. I always called home on my birthday, and it warmed my heart to hear the excitement in Khalil's voice when he greeted me. But this time, after the call ended, I entered the cell as though in a fog. As I walked to the sink to wash my hands, our conversation continued to play in my mind.

"Where's your mom?" I'd asked after about ten minutes. If my wife, Paula, didn't answer the phone, she was usually close enough for me to hear her voice. Normally, if Khalil didn't give up the phone within ten minutes, she'd demand it from him.

"Weeelll," my son had said in the singsong way children do when they're trying to remember something. "She went downstairs for a minute to talk to Auntie Chenelle."

I dried my hands, walked to the bunk and glanced at the date on my calendar: March 27, 2004. I looked at a happy picture of my son, his mother, and me together. Then I sat down, holding my head. I felt dizzy as I recalled more of my not-so-happy-birthday phone call.

"Dad, I have to tell you a secret, but you have to promise not to tell Mommy I told you. Okay?"

"Of course, I won't tell," I responded emphatically. I would never betray my boy. It was bad enough that I couldn't be with him every day. I couldn't walk him to school, take him to the park on weekends, or make it up to him after having to punish him. It seemed unfair that the limited interactions we did enjoy were predicated on the whims of his mother. As a result, trust became an even more treasured commodity between us.

"Mommy has a boyfriend, and she told me not to tell you!" He sounded more upset than I was. I did my best to console him and help him understand his mother's position, despite the burning betrayal I felt.

"Listen, Khalil, your mother is in a very difficult situation," I said. "I can't be there, and she probably feels lonely. It doesn't mean she loves you any less, or that she wants a new dad for you. I will always be your father. It's just hard for us to be together as much as we want to. Do you understand?"

"Yeah...but..." he started, his sentence trailing off.

"What's the matter?"

"I don't know...it's...'cause she said she still loves you."

"So how does your mother's friend treat you?" I asked, choosing to ignore the paradox he presented. I had no idea how to reconcile it in his mind, or mine, for that matter.

"Umm...Okay, but I don't talk to him really. He only comes over once or twice a week. I guess he's an okay guy."

Long after everyone had locked in and the officers had come around to count us, like chattel, I sat in the dark, seething. Although I'd had suspicions, it was so much different being face-to-face with reality. Before I knew it, I was in a fetal position crying myself to sleep.

The following days were increasingly difficult. I was tormented as I imagined my son playing with the hand grenade that just happened to be my heart:

"What's this thing for, Dad?"

"Don't pull tha...!"

Boom. Shrapnel.

It didn't surprise me to find out that my son's mother was involved with someone. Let's see: She was a beautiful young woman. Check. I hadn't seen her in over a year. Check. I wasn't receiving letters from her, not even birthday cards, and she was clearly avoiding me. Double check.

I could rationalize why she felt the need to escape from a relationship with a man in prison. It probably seemed to her that I was on another planet. Perhaps the few times we did see each other seemed more like dreams. Maybe when she went back to the real world, she needed to still have someone there.

On the other hand, if she truly loved me, wouldn't she be here for me, no matter what the circumstances? You know, "Ain't no mountain high enough," and all that. The more I thought about it, the more confused, angry, and frustrated I became. Even worse, I felt obliged to maintain my son's trust.

I couldn't directly confront her about her new friend without arousing suspicion that Khalil "dimed her out," for lack of a better phrase. Our communications were sparse at any rate, and I really wanted to see her in person. It seemed that wouldn't happen anytime soon.

I started to read all the old letters she had written to me because I hadn't detected any signs that she was tired; maybe there was something in writing that I had missed. But all I did was make myself angrier. Every other letter seemed to have an apology for not writing sooner and reassurances that I was always on her mind.

Maybe she was tired of thinking about me in prison. Maybe I just wasn't worth the effort, not even the effort to tell me that she couldn't do this anymore.

Whatever the case, all the beautiful things that she wrote in those letters now seemed meaningless. My favorite "Thinking of you" card, with the teddy bear sitting on a block of ice (the ice melted the longer she thought of me), the "I will always love you," the "I could never be with anyone but you"—they were all rendered null in my emotional universe; there was a black hole where my heart used to be.

What really stoked my ire was one letter that she wrote telling me she didn't want any of my ex-girlfriends to visit or even write me. Ain't that some shit? Here she was a few years later f@#$%*g some other dude but keeping me away from anyone she thought might take me away from her. Hypocritical, to say the least.

I really wanted to know what she was truly thinking and feeling. I got my opportunity four months later.

"Stephens—240—visit!"

Adrenaline flooded my body as the guard opened the cell gate. Every visit made me nervous. I didn't get visits from many people, so there was a strong likelihood that it was Paula and Khalil.

It was about 12:30 p.m. I rushed to take a quick shower and put on my visit greens and a shirt. I then waited impatiently for an escort to take me to the visiting room.

As I walked the corridors alongside an officer who shuffled like Frankenstein's monster, I thought about a friend of mine whose wife left him shortly after he came to prison. "I would probably melt if she came to see me right now, even after fifteen years," he said. I teased him mercilessly, calling him a "sucker for love." But at that moment, I felt like the sucker because I was excited at the prospect of seeing Paula, despite her indiscretions.

But after clearing security, I walked onto the visiting floor and spotted only Nicole, my wife's older sister, sitting by herself. I was even more nervous, as I walked over and gave her a hug and a kiss on the cheek.

"Oh my God, wussup!" she greeted me.

"Wassup, sis. How you been?" I hadn't seen Nicole since before my conviction, so it was good to see her. I just wanted to know why she was by herself, without her sister, or her two kids whom I'd always asked to see.

"I'm good," she said. "I brought the kids up to see you, too, but Paula didn't tell me I needed ID for them. She didn't even bring Khalil's ID, so she's outside waiting with them until I come out. They wouldn't let the kids in."

"Oh," I replied. I was dejected that I couldn't see the kids, especially my son. "For a minute there I thought something was wrong. I guess it's been so long since she's been here that she forgot the rules."

"Yeah," Nicole said. "I know it's been tough for you guys, but just give her some time. She's been really stressed out lately. Don't tell her I told you, but she hasn't been reading your letters because she starts crying."

Great. Another secret.

I had a lot of love for my wife's family, especially Nicole, because she had looked out for us on several occasions and always liked to see Paula and me happy. She had known me long enough to know that I really loved her sister, no matter what.

We spent the next hour catching up before Nicole got up to leave so Paula could come in.

"Just take care of yourself. Okay?" she said as she gave me a parting hug and kiss. "We'll see you again soon, and I'll send some pictures."

I stood there waving as she walked through the motorized gate that led to the waiting area outside of the visiting room. I felt the anger building up again as I thought about my son's mother abandoning me. But when I saw her practically running toward me with her arms outstretched, the venom melted away like cotton candy on the tip of a ravenous tongue.

She held me tightly for a long time, kissing my cheeks and lips in the way women do when they really miss you. I felt paralyzed in the face of such raw emotion. Finally, the guard instructed her to let me go. We sat down across the table/barrier that did nothing to block our mutual attraction.

As she gripped both my hands, I couldn't help admiring how beautiful she was, especially when she smiled. Yeah, I'm definitely a sucker. It didn't help that she was wearing my favorite color—red. I wasn't prepared for her attempt to hypnotize me.

"I know you're probably mad at me," she started. "But things have been hard lately."

"What do you mean?" I asked.

"Just the bills piling up and trying to save some money for school. Nicole came over this morning and said she wanted to come up here. If it wasn't for her, I don't know when I would be able to come see you."

"So why does it seem like I haven't been talking to you much lately?" I so badly wanted to add, "And, who's this dude you f@#%$*g wit'?!" But I thought about my informant, and I didn't want to blow his cover.

"I don't know...I've just had a lot on my mind." She didn't look at me when she said this. My insides felt hollow. "Khalil wanted to see you so bad, but I forgot his passport."

Then came this: "When is our next trailer?" She was referring to the extended, private visits prisoners are allowed to have with spouses, children, and certain other relatives every few months in trailers on prison grounds.

"I didn't request a date because I haven't heard from you," I told her.

There was nothing but silence and downcast eyes.

"I should have some money in a few months," she finally said. "And I'll be working steady through the week, so pick a weekend."

"Yeah, a'ight," I said. I could feel my conflicting emotions simmering. "If you need any money, let me know." As neo-slaves, prisoners don't make much money. But I could save some of what my mother and friends sent to at least pay for food for the trailer visit and for transportation for her to get to the prison.

We talked incessantly, mostly about our son. I continued to probe in order to figure out what she was really going through and why she had been missing in action for over a year.

"You know I still love you, but life isn't fair," was all I got. Before we knew it, visiting hours were over.

She held me tightly once more, promising that she would be there when I called, promising to write, promising that she would be there for the next trailer visit. "I love you," she mouthed, repeating words she had just whispered in my ear.

I'm definitely a sucker. I requested a calendar from the prison's Family Reunion Program (FRP) coordinator to pick a weekend date for a trailer. I thought that spending the weekend together would give us the opportunity to sort through everything we were feeling and that there would be no more secrets.

About a month after Paula's visit, I had a trailer date, but I was still having a hard time reaching Paula or Khalil. There were no letters, no visits. And the phone just kept ringing.

I was finally able to get through about a month later.

"Hi, Dad!" Khalil answered, as excited as ever.

"How have you been? I miss you."

"I'm okay, but I'm mad I couldn't see you when Mommy came with Auntie Nicole. I had to stay outside with my cousins," Khalil explained.

"I know. I was upset, too, but I have some good news. Your mom told me to pick a trailer date, and I got one for next month."

"Awwrriiight! Tell me the day so I can put it on the calendar."

We talked and laughed for about twenty minutes before I finally asked for his mother.

"Hold on. Let me go get her." I heard him knocking on the door, and then yelling. "Mom, my dad wants to talk to you!"

A few seconds later I heard her voice on the line.

"Yo, wussup?" she said quietly.

"I'm okay," I said. "I've been trying to reach you for a minute now, but you're never home."

"Yeah, I know," she responded curtly.

"Yo, what's wrong with you?" I asked.

"Nuthin'," she muttered unconvincingly.

"Anyway, I got that FRP date, and I'll send you some money next week for food and…"

"Um, yo, I have to go…. just talk to Khalil, okay? I have to go."

Just like that, she was gone, and I heard my son's voice again. "Heeeyyy, Dad."

"Hey, Khalil." The realization hit me. "Khalil, is your mother's friend there?"

"Yup, they're in her room smoking," he said, as though dying for me to ask.

"Oh." My emotions bubbled like lava. The supposed love of my life rounded on me for a blunt and some new dick.

Once I got off the phone, I could hardly think about anything else; I started reminiscing about all we had been through, Paula and I. We had known each other since she was fourteen years old, almost fifteen years; my mind was flooded with memories.

I remembered us cutting school to go to the movies or the park; holidays at the mall, and the first present she ever gave me (two connected wooden hearts she made with our names on them); her coming to visit me in the hospital when I got shot, and playing Ms. PacMan, in which I beat her only once or twice out of the thousands of games we played.

Most vividly, I remembered her decision to leave New York with me despite the fact that I was the prime suspect in a murder investigation. We moved to Florida, and got our first apartment off Fort Lauderdale's beach, where she tried to teach me how to float. I remembered the day our son was born and the day we got married.

Everything was good for us as we began building a life together—until the police came and took me away from her, from them.

I started to imagine how hard that must have been for her, how miserable she must have felt after I had been there for her every day, and then nothing—as if it had never happened, like a mirage in the Kalahari. Maybe it was unreasonable for me to think that she could be happy living like this, no matter how she felt about me.

Hadn't I been in prison for seven years and witnessed or heard about the suffocation of many relationships? I knew that many marriages failed. And I was convinced that prison added an extra burden that not everyone could bear. Prison could take something that was beautiful and damage it beyond recognition—like a dove on the ground unable to fly because of a broken wing, a firefly on a summer night without its dazzling light, or an ugly butterfly, bland without its captivating colors, flittering among dead flowers. For those who made it, God bless. Paula deserved better.

And what about my son and the difficulties he endured because of my incarceration? I know that his mother did her best, but a child needs both parents, especially in a city like New York. I was overwhelmed as I thought about statistics I had read about the high rate of incarceration among children whose parents were in prison.

Unbearable.

Khalil liked science and math. I imagined him growing up to be a scientist with his own lab, where he would discover unfathomable new life forms. Or maybe he would become a world-renowned mathematician and win the Nobel Prize for solving some mathematical quandary. Whatever it was, I just hoped he would be happy doing it, and that it was far away from any prison.

But who would be his role model? Who would teach him what it means to be a man? Was I even suitable to help him navigate the traps that life invariably offers, given my own improvidence? Would he think it was okay to come to prison because I did? How could I effectively discipline him when it was needed?

Several years ago, I was fortunate enough to participate in a parenting class offered by the Osborne Association, a nonprofit organization working to transform prisons from "human scrap heaps into human repair shops." I remembered our instructor, Annamarie Lewis, saying that although I could offer input from prison, discipline should be the province of the mother. The best that I could do was be the best role model I could be by encouraging Khalil with kind and forceful words when he did positive things, and by making it clear to him when I was disappointed with his behavior, which thankfully wasn't often.

Every father, I'm sure, wants to see himself in his children, but there were things in my life I never wanted Khalil to experience. How would I explain my imprisonment to my son?

On a trailer visit several years later Khalil asked me this: "Dad…how come you're in jail?" We were eating together at the kitchen table with my mother and sister, who had come up from Florida.

"When we finish eating, we'll go outside where you and I can talk," I said. I knew the question was coming. He had asked his mother on several occasions and she would just reply, "Ask your father when you see him."

After dinner, Khalil and I walked outside and sat alone on a swinging bench at the far end of the yard, surrounded by barbed wire fences and gun towers. No one else was outside. And just as I turned to face him, I thought I spotted a pale white butterfly flying low near a patch of dried grass.

"Khalil, you know that I love you and your mom very much and that I never wanted to leave you, right?"

"Uh huh," he said.

"Well," I said, eyeing him cautiously. "Before you were born, there was this guy in our neighborhood who didn't like your mother and me very much, and he specifically didn't like one of your mother's friends. You remember Aunt Keisha, right?"

"Yeah," he said, kicking his feet impatiently as we swung listlessly. Apparently, he had heard that part already.

"Anyway, things got out of control," I continued. "One day he tried to hurt your mom and threatened her and Aunt Keisha with a gun."

Khalil's feet stopped kicking.

"He also threatened me with a gun and so I shot him. He died on the spot."

"Oh," he said. I could see the gears turning in his head. "Couldn't you have called the police?"

"I don't think they could have helped. I feel that I did what I had to do to protect your mother and myself. I just wish I wasn't so angry during the whole ordeal. Maybe if I had a clear head, I could have found a way to end the animosity before it was too late.

"Sometimes we get so caught up in our emotions that we lose sight of what's really important. It's hard to see someone's point of view when you're caught up in your own fear, or jealousy, or anger. Do you understand?"

"Yeah, I understand," he said. "But where did you get a gun?"

"Well, that's another story for another day. Come on, let me show you how to shoot a jumper before it gets dark."

"Okay!"

We spent the night talking and playing basketball, chess, and video games until he fell asleep on my shoulder. I scooped him up, carried him to a small bedroom and lay him on the bed, where he could sleep comfortably. It was one of the few times I could actually tuck him in, and I savored the moment. He was a beautiful child of Jamaican and Trinidadian ancestry, with long eyelashes and curly hair. From a chair next to the bed, I just sat there watching him sleep as he sprawled out, marking the entire bed as his territory.

I wondered if he knew how much he meant to me. Did he know how much my heart changed from the moment I knew that his mother was pregnant? Did he know that for me he represented a true chance at redemption, a chance to be free of the apathy and frustration that secretly corroded my insides? I doubted it, but for now the thought of him dreaming about the day he spent with his father was enough.

⁂

"Hi, Dad," my son answered the phone somberly.

"Khalil, what's the matter?"

"Well ... you can't tell Mom I told you. Okay?"

Here we go again.

"The other day she was fighting."

"With who?"

"Her boyfriend," he said matter-of-factly.

"Oh, you mean they were arguing?"

"Noooo. He pushed her real hard, and then she punched him in the face and he started bleeding."

"Where were you when this was happening?"

"I was playing video games."

"Are you okay?" I asked. "Is your mom okay?"

"Yeah, she made him leave and told him not to come back."

We had a long talk about how he felt seeing his mother in that situation, and about how oftentimes grown people have disagreements but should never hit each other.

"Dad...you think because you always get As in school the people will let you come home soon?"

"I...."

"Yeah, 'cause mom always says she misses you and that you wouldn't fight with her like that. I told her I already know you wouldn't do that anyway."

"Nah, but maybe I'd put her over my knee and spank her from time to time."

At that, he chuckled.

"Seriously, though, Khalil, I want you to know that no matter what happens I will always love you and your mom. No matter what."

"I know Dad ... I love you, too."

"Good, but don't tell your mother what I said." That would be my own little secret.

Kenneth R. Brydon

A Course in Reconciliation

In Loving Memory of My Father, Loy Brydon

I T WAS ABOUT 2:00 IN THE MORNING on May 7, 1978, when I stood on a freeway overpass in Thousand Oaks, California, and looked down on the two northbound lanes of Highway 101. At nineteen, I had only two friends: bitterness and anger. I had done what "I could never" do. The only part of a Bible verse I could recall was an "eye for an eye." The words were a whisper telling me that jumping was the right thing to do.

Traffic wasn't much. The bright lights of street lamps flashed off the hoods of the cars occasionally passing below. Each one was accompanied by a sharp thrumming noise as they shot out from underneath my feet. I felt as if I was being sucked over the side—all I had to do was let go. I thought about how my Uncle Glen had killed himself. He'd also chosen an overpass on Highway 101, in Everett, Washington, as his final destiny. Maybe he'd faced the southbound lanes. The spring air was warm and smelled slightly of diesel. Uncle Glen hadn't killed anyone; what more reason did I need to give myself to the same fate.

My brother Mark really flipped out when Uncle Glen died. But, at six years old, I hadn't known him well, and it didn't seem to matter. Maybe I didn't care about others. But what was this dark cloud of guilt crushing the life out of me?

There was no one left to blame, no one around to stop me. For someone who had caused so much pain and destruction, this was as good an ending as any. It was time I turned that rage on the one who deserved it in the first place. "God have mercy!" I whispered.

The street below wanted me; it would all be over with a quick move. God, I almost killed my brother the week before! Mark's face was beaten to a pulp. I couldn't hurt anyone else; no more confusion, no more … "God have mercy."

An inner voice screamed for me to jump; I leaned forward on the rail, my hands braced on top. But the moment suddenly collided with a new reality—an absurd idea only an hour ago.

"I'll get help!" came out of my mouth.

I turned and walked down from the overpass toward a closed gas station. I knew a guy who'd done a year in prison for multiple armed robberies. "I'll do about four for this," I reasoned. "I'll get help, change my life."

A pay phone received my dime to call the police and turn myself in.

On the north side of the Golden Gate Bridge on Highway 101, about ten miles along, a sign before a freeway off-ramp says "San Quentin State Prison." During my father's drive up from Fresno, California, in late summer 1995, I imagine that he took that off-ramp. My half-brother Ty was in the car with him.

As I arrived at the visiting room entrance, the smell of buttered popcorn wafted from the room. "Visit!" I said to the prison guard on the other side of the door.

He looked me over as he opened the door. "You been out here before?" he asked.

"I've been seeing my wife twice a week for the last two years," I said, looking up at the ceiling and turning around with my arms out wide as he gave me a pat search.

He finished his search with a light tap on both my ankles. "Okay," he said, leaving me to walk in without telling me the rules I already knew.

The visiting room was two-thirds as long as a football field and half as wide. Three rows of knee-high tables ran its length, with chairs on both sides. The noise level was a constant of many voices intermixed with loud shrieks of young children who wanted more attention.

Dad stood with Ty at the far end from me. I gave my prison ID to a guard at the podium and walked the length to where they were. Both smiled as I approached. But my eyes were on my father, whose face revealed a still-fresh pain.

"Hi, Dad," I said, hugging him.

"Hi, son," he said in his deep voice.

We stood with arms on each other's shoulders, quietly sharing the joy of seeing each other after a year. But our strong grips on each other's shoulders spoke the reason for the visit. His gray eyes misted, but he remained as I knew him.

"Hey, bro," I said, turning to Ty.

"Kenny," he said, hugging me. Ten years younger, he lived in Arizona, as did Dad. About ten years ago, when he was a teenager, he started writing to me, wanting to know his "lifer" brother. We'd written and I'd called through the years.

In some ways, I felt a very deep connection to him. Perhaps too many of my letters were more like sermons about God and sobriety, but he was always glad to talk with me on the phone.

Ty was a prison guard in Arizona. He'd come to visit me ten months ago. As a clerk for a captain, I'd managed to swing Ty a tour of the inside of San Quentin with a lieutenant.

We picked out three seats against the wall before heading to the vending machines. I got several hugs from other people's visitors, who were part of a collective visiting room family that my wife, Bettye, and I belonged to. We would all play cards and Scrabble, and even embarrassed each other with cakes and crowds singing, "Happy Birthday!"

But this time, their greetings were subdued; they gave gentle nods to both my father and brother. A fellow lifer and his wife grinned as they looked at me, then Dad, then Ty. "Don, Kathy," I said to them as we passed by.

I pointed to what I wanted from the vending machine. Dad began feeding in the dollar bills that I wasn't allowed to touch. "What were they all grins about?" Dad asked, nodding back to the couple.

I chuckled. "They see how much we look alike," I said, pulling my roast beef sandwich out of the machine.

Dad looked back at them a moment, and then he grinned. He stood 5'8" to my 5'6", and Ty stood 5'10". I used to rag on Dad about why he'd picked Mom, who was only 4'10", when Ty's mother, Tee, was 5'6".

All three of us were broad-shouldered, thick-chested, and had well-defined jaw lines. We all had voices as deep as the Sha Na Na baritone, Bowser. A tattoo of a black panther marked Dad's left forearm, with its claws digging into his skin. Vietnam veterans doing time with me also had that panther; they'd only give me a pained smile when I asked what it represented. Dad wouldn't explain it, either.

"Kenny," Ty said, "you want a soda?" He was already walking to the soda machine as I asked for a Dr. Pepper. We'd stepped to another machine when Ty came back. "What's with the handcuffs?" he asked.

I looked over my shoulder to an area next to the visitors' entrance and saw an older fellow with his hands cuffed behind him. A prison guard securely held onto one of his arms. "He's on death row," I said.

My brother nodded as he studied the well-groomed inmate in the same denim blue clothes as mine. The condemned see visitors in a space away from the rest of us, in a secure cubicle large enough to seat four people, without the cuffs.

"I got that clipping you sent," I told him. It was a photo of Ty in his uniform standing guard during a commutation hearing for an Arizona condemned inmate. Ty said he really didn't like being there.

My brother gave the manacled man another brief look, and then he turned back my way. I thought I saw Ty shudder.

Carrying my food back to our seats, I sat down with my back to the wall and my father and brother across from me. "How was the trip?"

Dad didn't hesitate. "Other than Ty being a real pain in the ass, it was alright!"

Ty turned a bit red. "Yeah," he answered, "and you wouldn't even stop for a minute!" It was a family moment. Dad never stopped when he took a trip, and Ty wanted to stop for a beer.

We ate in silence for a moment before Dad began. "The funeral went well," he said. "Your brother Kevin shared a poem, and Mary asked a pastor of a local church to speak." Dad paused, looking at me. "He did a good job."

I thought about asking about the pastor, but Dad went on. "Your mother was there with your sister Cathy." My sister was from my mother's second marriage. Dad's voice suddenly shifted as he said quickly, "Mary had Mark cremated."

I felt my stomach twist. A body lying in a coffin somehow didn't seem so absolutely dead, but there was no debating a pile of ashes. Pushing past the point, I asked, "How's Mary taking it?"

Dad took a deep breath. "Well," he said, "she seems okay."

I nodded and turned to Ty. "How're the kids?"

"Getting big," he said.

"How's Hugh?" I asked about my other half-brother.

"Dad went to see Hugh perform," Ty said.

I raised my eyebrows at that. "Really?" I asked. "Did you bring earplugs?"

Dad laughed. "I should have."

For a while, we talked of family still living. Ty's four kids were the only grandkids Dad had. Our sandwiches finished, Ty stood up. "I'm going to go talk to them," he said, pointing to the prison guards I'd introduced him to on his last visit.

A couple very close to Bettye and me stopped in front of where we sat.

"Dad, you remember Rusty and Diana?"

He looked up at them. "Yeah, sure," he said, standing to shake their hands.

"We're very sorry for you," Diana said.

Dad nodded. "Thank you."

They gave me a caring look. I smiled and nodded as they walked away, and then watched as my father sat back down. When he looked at me, I began a scripted conversation. "Dad, what are you going to do?"

Dad's face went hard a moment, and then he looked down before speaking in a calm voice. "Well, I'm going to drive Ty home, and then I'm going back to Fresno and check things out for myself."

I felt my heart flutter at his words. He looked up at me again; his face was blank. I looked away, reaching for my soda, trying to keep my hand from shaking. I shouldn't speak my next words. Yet, it now fell on me; it was what a first-born ought to do. A weight pressed on my mind and heart. I spoke for all five sons, living and now dead.

"I don't think you want to be my cellmate, Dad."

There wasn't any hesitation in his answer. "No one does that to my son!"

Prison is where you need to know a real threat from empty words, and seventeen years inside had taught me how to distinguish between the two. Adrenalin had my heart beating fast; it felt like a riot was kicking off around me.

Seeing past my own pain over Mark's death, I'd considered how the rest of the family might react. Mom would only be able to bury herself in a bottle, but Dad would not find solace in such passive ways.

Dad was a "man's man." A book in the San Quentin Library on the history of skydiving documented him as the first American to log over a thousand free-fall jumps, and told of his pioneering work in the testing of parachute designs. While he was putting together the Golden Knights Army Parachute Team at Fort Bragg, North Carolina, I was born in the hospital.

A master sergeant in the Green Berets, he fought in some of the hottest battle zones in two tours of Vietnam. A Purple Heart recipient, he risked his own life to rescue then Navy Lieutenant John Kerry from a booby trap.

My father sat across from me, his eyes wide. His shock slowly ebbed as he considered that I understood his intentions. I finally broke the tension-filled silence. "Let the legal system deal with them, Dad."

He leaned forward, bringing his head halfway over the table between us, and spoke in a hushed voice that was still impossibly deep. "I don't want those fuckers alive! I want them dead!"

Among the hats Dad wore in the Army was drill instructor; a private would have been shaking in terror. He pointed a finger at the table as if it were responsible. "I'm going to tie them to a tree, and they're going to see what I can do with a knife!"

He pulled back, sitting upright and looking around the visiting room with his jaw clenched and his strong hands opening and closing. "They're going to die like dogs. Just like they left my son!"

When he'd finished, I continued my prepared words. "You know, Dad, prison is full of people who've done just what you're thinking about."

He raised his eyebrows as he looked at me. It was a long moment before a slight grin turned up the sides of his mouth and he asked, "What are you going to do, turn me in?"

I shrugged at his comment and grabbed my soda. "There are no perfect crimes," I said, pointing around the room to remind him of where we were having our conversation.

He sat there resting elbows on his knees, his hands grasping, still trying to take hold of what wasn't there to satisfy his bloodlust. I waited, glancing over at Ty, who was enjoying his time talking shop with the visiting room officers.

A moment later, Dad's shoulders dropped slightly. "I know Mark wasn't a saint," he said, with difficulty, "but he didn't deserve that."

"I know how you feel, Dad, but maybe you should consider this: There's a family out there that hates me; they feel the way you do." My heart was heavy as I looked at my father. "Would you like them to do to me what you want to do to them?"

Perhaps the idea of my being assaulted stirred up more anger. He took several deep breaths and looked around the room. Then he leaned forward and exhaled, and stared at the ground a moment. "I hear what you're saying, son," he said, bringing his head up.

Dad's jaw was still tight when Ty returned. My brother looked at me and then at our father. "What's up?" he asked.

As Ty looked at Dad, my father was staring intently at me. I grinned slightly and said, "On the way back, Dad's going to stop and you two are going to toast Mark with a beer."

"Really?" he asked, looking from Dad to me.

My father glared at me. He was pissed.

Lise Porter

Bitter, Candy-Coated Lipstick

MY MOTHER WAS TAKEN TO JAIL on December 14, the day before her sixty-second birthday. The sheriff came with no apparent warning, but my mom must have known that the police would eventually arrest her. After all, she had stashed away $700 in cash in a locked filing cabinet in case she needed it while incarcerated.

Still, her apartment had been left in chaos. Food rotted in the fridge; bills remained on her desk unpaid. Unwrapped Christmas gifts cluttered the floor. Paper, ribbons, and boxes were everywhere.

The apartment posed a problem. When my mother was previously incarcerated, I didn't intervene and she lost all her possessions—photographs, furniture, pots and pans, and clothes. She had to start over from scratch. I couldn't do that to her again. Even though this was the fifth time she'd serve jail time for driving under the influence of alcohol, I decided I'd help this time. I knew if she lost everything again, it would kill her.

A friend familiar with the effects of addiction volunteered to help me. We went to the apartment together and began the laborious process of going through legal and personal documents—shredding some, filing away others—sorting through bank statements, divorce papers, and my childhood report cards (straight As). We threw away perishable food, washed dishes left in the sink, gathered photographs and her $700 cash. I found the money order she had left me for Christmas, but I decided not to go through the unwrapped presents. Then we spoke to the landlord, and paid the next month's rent.

But after the holidays, when it was time to thoroughly go through the apartment and put things in storage, I couldn't do it. I bordered on a nervous breakdown. I wondered how many incarcerations she'd go through and how much more she'd rely on me in the future, if I intervened in this way.

She wasn't dead, yet I'd have to go through her things as if she were. And I didn't want the responsibility. I refused to be my mother's keeper.

My friend and I told the landlord that we were handing over the keys. I drafted a letter legally releasing the apartment and her belongings. I cried while I spoke with the property manager.

"This isn't the first time you've been through this, is it?" she asked, squeezing my hand. I cried even more.

We didn't know when my mom would be released. She was to be sentenced in February, so the landlord said he'd keep the apartment for her until then. After all, she'd been a good tenant and the landlord sympathized with her situation. She suffered from an addiction and depression; she wasn't a criminal.

But her release kept being pushed back—March, May, it was always up in the air—until we finally got a definite date, July 11. Miraculously, the landlord had agreed to hold the apartment and waive the rent, as an act of generosity. It was a lesson to me: When you don't try to "fix" everything, God often takes care of it for you.

When I heard about the landlord's goodwill, I wrote my mom a letter telling her the news. She could return to her apartment. But I don't think the information registered in her consciousness. By then, I think, she had already decided to take her own life.

All the time my mom was in jail, she didn't know that her apartment and belongings had been kept intact. Earlier, I had told her that I had handed over responsibility to the landlord. She'd initially been okay with this, knowing it wasn't my job. Then she seemed to forget and began to freak out.

I had visited her in jail every weekend for a month, but she was hysterical the last time I ever saw her. It was such a horrible visit that I never went back.

She barely acknowledged me. She pulled at her trousers, showing off how much weight she had lost. Then she pointed to her face proudly, delighted that she had scored some makeup.

"You know how I got the lipstick?" she said, giggling like a maniacal clown.

"No," I said wearily. She had not even said hello to me.

"I bought jawbreakers from the commissary and ran them under hot water. The dye bled off and I put it on my lips."

I had spent three hours of my day to visit, and she didn't seem to even care that I was there.

My Al-Anon sponsor had told me, "Just because she's doing time, you don't have to." So I stopped visiting. I did it to save myself emotionally.

It wasn't the first time I'd sought self-preservation in this way. I did not make the ten-hour drive when she was incarcerated at the state prison. For better or for worse, I just couldn't do it.

Other times, I hadn't protected myself, like during her first incarceration when I was twenty-four. I had flown down from San Francisco to San Diego to see her right before Christmas. It had been a jarring experience seeing my mom's big brown eyes, as forlorn as Bambi's, looking back at me through the glass wall.

And there was another visit a few years ago. That time, I went with the man she lived with, Bob. He had a codependent allegiance to her, sparing me the ordeal of her unpaid bills and putting money on her books so she could buy basic things like shampoo and stamps.

When my mom faced Bob and me through the glass, I saw depression plastered all over her face. "Isn't it terrible?"

she kept repeating over and over again, staring at me as if I could fix it. Yet I wasn't even certain she saw me, or knew it was me. I felt I could have been anyone.

Bob, sensing she'd be depressed, brought out some photographs of the plastic dolls she owned and called by name. At her most neurotic, she drove them around in the back seat of her car and talked to them as if they were real. I always wondered if this was her way of regressing to happier times when she played with dolls as a child. As she looked at the photos, I was astonished to see my mom's face suddenly illuminated and transformed. "My babies! Lise, see my babies. Bob brought me my babies." And then she proceeded to name them all, cooing and cooing at the pictures in the most surreal way.

What about me? I wanted to scream. *I'm your baby; I'm your baby! WHAT ABOUT ME?!*

Bob became terminally ill and died before my mom's two-year prison sentence expired. It broke her heart.

I decided that no matter how much I wanted to be the good daughter, I had to stop the visits. I knew there would be the risk of her attempting suicide when she got out, but I'd taken that chance many times.

Many people saw my mother's trajectory as inevitable. A former boyfriend once said, "You know the other shoe is going to drop. One of these days you're going to get the call that she is in the ER, has had an accident, or has committed suicide. The shoe is going to drop."

It dropped, all right.

Upon her release in July, we'd arranged to meet, but she left me a vague voicemail message saying she wasn't going to come. She said she was depressed. I had no contact information for her, no way to reach her. This pattern of behavior was not new, but the suicide note I received in the mail two days later was.

As I pulled bills from the mailbox, I discovered an envelope with my mom's familiar handwriting. I opened the envelope, and my deepest fears unfolded.

7/11/08

Dear Lise,

I live in a world of utter darkness, despair and pain. I cannot stand life anymore. There seems to be no way out. Depression has totally overcome me. I can barely walk. When I am gone you will not have any more worries or concerns and will be free to carry on your life without any more pain from me. I am very sorry I was such a terrible mother. Please forgive me. I love you very much—too much to cause you any more grief. I hope the rest of your life is filled with great happiness and love. Please understand that I am very mentally ill and can no longer cope.

I love you,
Mom

I felt sick to my stomach. My mom had attempted suicide twelve years earlier, after she was released the first time. A prison social worker had expressed concern, but they released her anyway, two days after Christmas and a week after her birthday. She jumped from her apartment balcony, breaking a few ribs and puncturing a lung. She lived in chronic pain after that, furthering her addiction to alcohol and painkillers.

But I'd never received a letter like this before. Something about the letter felt frighteningly like a final goodbye.

I groped for a timeline in my mind. She was released from jail on Friday, July 11. The letter was postmarked the same day, with Las Colinas as the return address. I received the letter on Monday night, July 13. I prayed her frame of mind had changed and that she would soon contact me, maybe from a psychiatric hospital. Maybe she had gotten a grip. I clung to this as much as I secretly wished that maybe this time would finally be "it"—that the roller coaster of fear was going to end. I didn't want my mom to die, but the constant ups and downs of her depression and instability were killing me.

Still emotionally frantic and on the verge of hysteria, I called my neighbor and family for support. Then I called the police, and they gave me the medical examiner's telephone number. I thanked them as if this were everyday polite conversation. I dialed the number and they told me they didn't have any unidentified bodies at the moment. I don't know how I slept that night.

The next morning, I made a cup of coffee and began making calls. I called anyone and everyone I could think of who might have heard from my mom. But the list wasn't long, as she'd burned so many bridges.

The day had a surreal quality to it, as if time had stopped and I was floating through time and space as slow as molasses. That morning, I sat looking at my mom and dad's wedding pictures. I looked at her happy, pretty face shining back at me in black and white with the same awe I felt as a child. I touched the photographs, trying to feel my mom through the plastic covering of the album page, knowing on a cellular level that I would never see her again. I walked around the house and cried, looking at things that reminded me of her. At one point in the afternoon, I stepped outside for a walk. I found myself suddenly stopping after passing a particular tree. A breeze blew up and I felt compelled to turn back and touch its trunk. I put my cheek against the bark and found myself hugging it. I wondered if it was my mom. I felt a Presence, strongly trying to reassure me despite my knowing she was gone.

But I didn't have any proof that she was actually dead. And there had been many, many occasions where I had thought my mom was dead and she wasn't. Experience had taught me that addicts have many lives and that every time you think they're gone, they're not. So I could only think that she was still alive. So I could function.

My boss had called at noon, as I'd informed her of the situation. But how many days could I take off from work? I was told no news was good news and that if she were dead, I would have probably heard by now.

I went back to work the next day and tried to go on with life as normal.

Truth is, nothing had been normal about the past nine months since the sheriff, with a warrant for her arrest, came to her apartment the day before her sixty-second birthday. There is nothing normal about incarceration.

People often say addicts have to hit rock bottom. That until they do, they can't recover. But I don't know that jail helped my mom any. The criminalization of her addiction deepened her sense of shame and poor self-esteem, causing her to drink more. It shattered any sense of dignity she had left.

True, life with my mom during my teen and adult years had been difficult. But every time I looked at her suicide note, I winced at the words "I'm sorry I've been such a terrible mother."

She was far from a terrible mother. When I was little, she was actually a very good mom. She always fed, clothed and bathed me, read me stories, and went out of her way to delight me. She never raised her voice or called me names. She was kind and gentle. Fragility and fear proved to be the fatal flaws driving her to drink. By the time I was in the fourth grade, alcoholism had left her emotionally unavailable. As the years progressed, so did her drinking.

As I got older, I learned that no matter how much I tried, nothing I did or didn't do could alter the course of my mom's actions or her depression. But here I was now with a suicide note in hand.

What if I would never have the chance to see her again? What if the last time I saw her was behind a plate of glass, her eyes both wild and sad and her mouth smeared with the red dye of jawbreakers?

After returning to work, I went through the motions for two days, compartmentalizing. I glided along like a duck on a pond; underneath I paddled like hell. After work, I swam, my senses and memories heightened as I propelled my body through the water, the pool a large amniotic sac. Then as I walked out to the parking lot with wet hair and my gym bag, I couldn't help noticing mothers and daughters. I thought of my mother when she used to pick me up from various places: Girl Scouts, catechism, school, day care. I remembered holding her hand as we crossed parking lots, traipsing along beside her, telling her about my day and what I wanted for dinner. I remembered being close to my mom, sitting on the couch as she read aloud to me and I glanced at the words on the page, subconsciously teaching myself to read.

Those thoughts were the only thing that soothed me.

Just when I'd come to think my mom was alive, the call came late Friday morning. Almost a week had passed with no news, and I'd started to breathe easy. Until I heard an unfamiliar man's voice over the phone ask, "Is this Lise Porter?"

I'd gotten calls like this before. Some hospital nurse or doctor informing me that she was in the ER. I waited, half-expecting to hear the news that, yes, she was still alive but was in a hospital somewhere. The man didn't follow the script. Instead he told me that she was dead.

She'd been alive up until the previous night. Shopkeepers had seen her milling in front of their stores the day before. They thought she was homeless.

She was found dead on the street, in front of the stores. The police reassured me there had been no foul play. Pills were scattered around her, and a few were in a little plastic bag with her booking number on it. She died from acute intoxication of amitriptyline, a medication given for sleep and to calm nerves. The jail had apparently released her with these pills.

She had on her a list of family addresses and phone numbers, which is how they contacted me. She also had Microsoft Word certificates from computer program tutorials she had successfully completed in jail. What was missing was my headshot photo that I had made sure she'd carried. My aunt said she wouldn't have been able to go through with her actions if she'd had my photo on her.

Without a doubt, my mom made a choice. She'd made it a week ago when she wrote the note. Perhaps even before then. I know she made a choice because I had made arrangements to help her. I guaranteed that she had the maximum amount of money on her books two days before her release so that she could get a taxicab to a motel or her apartment. I had written her that I would meet her the day after her release with her purse, driver's license, and money orders for $3,000. I was buying her car at blue book value, as we'd arranged, which would give her some cash. Her apartment was miraculously preserved for her. Her landlord waived her rent for nine months. I had given her the number of an excellent rehabilitation program that was free and provided counseling for people getting out of prison. And in my last note to her I had said, "I love you."

I knew she had made a choice because she didn't show up for her money and she didn't make an appointment to have her hair colored, as she always did when she was released from jail.

Two days after my mother's memorial service, I received a phone call with another unfamiliar man's voice.

"I'm trying to contact Mary Hoffman."

"Who is this?"

"I'm her probation officer. Do you know where I can reach her?"

I choked on tears of anger. "She committed suicide a few days after she got out of jail," I said, blaming the man with the tone of my voice.

"I'm so sorry."

He was sorry. I could tell. But was the system sorry? The district attorney, the one who called my mom a "menace to society" and looked at her like she was a cockroach before she was sentenced to two years at Chowchilla—was she sorry?

My mom had to wear an orange jumpsuit one too many times. Sure, her own behaviors and choices put her there. But she was sick, not a criminal. If she had had health insurance every time her blood alcohol level was so high it almost killed her, she would have been transferred from a hospital ER to a psychiatric hospital and put on a seventy-two-hour hold for a suicide attempt. And if she had had more money, she might have been able to hire a decent attorney. Perhaps then she might have been sentenced to a rehabilitation program instead of jail five different times.

Jail not only humiliated my mom, it humiliated me. It put a wedge between us. If I'd been able to visit her in a hospital, to meet with a social worker, attend a family therapy session—anything other than looking through that plate of glass and speaking to my mom on a telephone would have been more helpful. We were both victims to the haphazardness of the system, never knowing when her court or release dates would be because they constantly changed.

I can handle the trauma of my mom's suicide better than I can handle the trauma of her incarceration. They have books and support groups for dealing with the former. No one talks about the latter. In fact, every time she went to jail, it was like a death. Every time she went away, I was left with no mother to spend the holidays with and with apartments and legal matters to tend to, as one does after a death.

Jail, as much as her suicide, killed her.

A week or two after my mom's death, I found one of her letters to me still lying around. I had tried to put them all away but had missed this one. She wrote that she'd soon have a release date but ended the letter abruptly. "We are going to have an emergency raid so I will have to close for now. I think they are looking for drugs. Love, Mom."

Scott Gutches

Walk, Don't Run

I COMMITTED MY CRIME long before I met Karen. Back then, my heart was poisoned against myself, and misery was like a flannel blanket in January, well used and comfortable.

I hadn't always been that way, and I'm not that way anymore. But at the time, although it may not have been healthy or just, I existed like that in order to live a semi-normal life; I had to ignore what I'd done and move on.

Still, I couldn't sleep at night, a side effect of swallowing your conscience and washing it down with silence. It was not an easy way to live—like self-administering daily inoculations for an incurable illness for so long that you could barely remember when you didn't need them to live.

It didn't help that my emotional growth had been stunted by neglect and, dare I say, abuse. I had expectations and deluded beliefs about love; when my own experience did not match up, I lied to myself—"Everything is fine; we're completely happy"—to avoid dismantling a mutually abusive marriage.

It may seem shocking, but the thought of initiating the separation from an abusive partner was not part of my psychological vocabulary. So when I learned that it was not only okay to leave, but my right and responsibility, I felt like a man blind since birth who could finally see the color spectrum.

I survived my own emotional ignorance and learned what a relationship was supposed to be: nurturing, caring, and taking joy in each other's personal growth. I learned about "red flags" and the importance of basing relationships on this healthy model instead of past, failed ones. I was proud when I noticed the warning signs in subsequent budding relationships and ended them tactfully and judiciously. I was making healthy choices; it felt good.

But finding the right person for a healthy relationship is difficult. Let's face it; by the mid-thirties, everyone you meet is someone else's leftovers, narrator included and at the top of the list. We all have baggage, and I admit I brought the seven-piece deluxe set with two overstuffed carry-ons. But I packed them myself. I wasn't choosey or checking whether women I had relationships with could schlep their own, or more important, if all of our crap could fit in the same trunk.

So successful relationships still eluded me. I suspected my hidden past was interfering with my ability to completely give myself over to another. There was always that voice saying, "She wouldn't be with you if she knew what you've done. Guilt counts for nothing. No one believes you're sorry!" It seemed that the more I tried to push my past away from my conscience, the farther I pushed myself away from people.

Three years after my marriage had come undone, I found myself 600 miles away from my children, living as though I were in a fraternity, in a job I hated and a career I despised, in a place I would never call home. It wasn't long before everything began to wear thin.

I don't know why some people must make every mistake imaginable, go down every wrong path, break from every moral and ethical standard, and live a life that makes absolutely no sense in order to get it right, to see the right path, to get back to a solid sense of right and wrong, to put things in order.

It dawned on me that I needed to go home, back to my kids, and resume the life I was supposed to have. I made a promise to my kids that I would move back home within a year. Time was running out, but I resolved to make good on it.

To live up to that promise, I needed to be whole, so I could be useful to them. And the only way to do that was to go on as though nothing had happened. I had to see my past as a glitch, an egregious error of the human condition. My guilt and shame needed to take a back seat. If I carried them with me, I'd be useless as a father. Looking back, it was the most decisive I've ever been in my entire life.

Not too long after deciding to be closer to my kids, I received a job offer. I would go from a substantial salary of nearly six digits to making less than $15 an hour. It took all of about ten minutes to take the job. It was the best decision I made in my entire occupational life. It was a job I enjoyed.

I was living near my children and seeing them on an even split with my ex-wife. I had a small basement apartment and furnished it second-hand from the Salvation Army. Financially, it was a struggle, but I found it easier as a lifestyle. I no longer cared if the kids spilled food on the couch I had gotten for free, or if they scratched the TV stand that had cost $25. I couldn't take them out to dinner as often, but I was surprised at how much I enjoyed cooking for them. Instead of distancing from them, I drew even closer, doing arts and crafts, teaching them college-level vocabulary words, and going over homework.

I was there for Cub Scouts and Girl Scouts and went to parent-teacher meetings. I took absolute joy in my children. For most healthy people, this is no revelation. But for someone deeply rooted in dysfunction, it was as though cataracts had been removed and I was in awe of the clarity and beauty of the simple things in life.

I met Karen at the very beginning of this new life I'd created for myself. Beautiful, intelligent, light-hearted, wholesome—a woman complete in herself, independent but not impenetrable. She didn't need a man in her life; she just wanted one. It was apparent that I could finally have a healthy relationship, and it would be with her.

The feeling of falling in love is a momentary condition. Personal boundaries and emotional inhibitions seem to fall away freely; souls diffuse into one. Then real love begins, and the opportunity for a meaningful partnership. This is when you choose to be with—rather than "ending up" with—someone.

I chose to be with Karen. Turns out, she was the best decision I'd made, one I'm quite proud of, and one that would prove to save my life.

Our love affair was like nothing I'd known, but everything a perfect romance could be: companionship, friendship, contentment, and fondness for each other. But it's easy to have these things when you're at your best—when life is free of discord, and trivial worries remain trivial, with no simmering resentment needed to be kept at bay. We spent the time we had wrapped around each other. We tried desperately to hold each second captive.

I don't know much about grace, but I like to think that it was grace that made sense of my life just before my fall. It was too synchronous to consider it coincidence. Something awful was headed my way. My mistakes were conspiring to exact the justice they were due. But here was life showing me what it was always supposed to be like, perhaps so I wouldn't forget through the retribution I would surely receive. In my mind, it was nothing less than a gift to preserve my heart in future times and in future places where the hearts of men grow cold and calloused.

Don't ask me how, but I knew I was going to be arrested. I thought about running. Everything important to me was about to be taken away, so what did I have to lose by making a getaway? Well, to be precise, everything important in my life —my children, Karen, my brother, friends. The likelihood of their walking away was high; they had a choice. I could face that, but not ever seeing them again, not knowing where they were or how they were doing for the rest of my life, and their not knowing what became of me was not an option. I did not know how I was going to face the music, but I knew I was going to.

I found myself in jail facing the consequences I'd long been avoiding and denying. It's profound how instantly you can summarize and weigh your losses. When faced with doom, especially when you know you deserve it, you cannot help erasing all hope from your life. It also makes you question whether you deserved any of the joy you had extracted between that point and the transgressions that got you there.

You begin to fear that those who loved you and called you friend will think that all the goodness in you was just a mask, hiding all of your nefarious plots against the world; your laugh, your smile, your intentions are now all suspect.

With your humanity in doubt, you resign yourself to be eternally despised. Who, after all, could love such a monster? What will Karen, my children, my friends, my family think of me when they find out? What will they think of themselves?

I made no phone calls. The days passed with the despair of waiting for biopsy results, except you're praying for the sweet solace of a fast death. My brother would tell me later that once you're falling, you can't tell which way is up until you've hit the bottom. You can't ascend until you have a fixed point as your guide. The bottom force-feeds your consciousness; because it is the darkest, it makes even the weakest light seem brilliant.

That's what it was like when Karen came to see me. She visited after my brother did what I'd asked him to: tell her that the man she loved was real and not fictional. She was obviously torn to pieces, but she was there. Her love was unwavering, shining and burning like the sun emerging from an eclipse. Her love was unexpected and blinded my eyes, heretofore fixated on the mesmerizing blackness.

She didn't run.

When I was out on bond before my sentencing, I took Karen to climb Mt. Bierstadt in Colorado, an easy hike but 14,000 feet in elevation nonetheless. She'd had surgery a few weeks before and wasn't sure she could handle it. But I didn't care; I told her we'd go as high as she could. About halfway up, she decided she couldn't go on. I pulled her aside and gave her a bracelet. It was one she'd admired at a Swarovski store a few weeks earlier.

"This is for going with me as far as you could," I said. She knew I was talking about life as well as the mountain.

Karen and I had different reasons to run, physically and emotionally. Yet what held us together was sharing the same reasons to stay. We're still together today, just over a year later, because today is all we have—no matter how far apart we are or how much razor-wire and concrete separate us.

If anything causes us to break and run, it won't be because of a major catastrophe—and prison won't have anything to do with it. Like in any relationship, it is a lack of attention that allows people to slowly drift apart.

The journey is too long to concentrate on the destination. Just like on Mt. Bierstadt, if we make the destination our goal, we'll miss the opportunities along the way to enjoy each other's companionship. We'll forget why we're walking side by side.

Joel Williams

Huero and Mike

I LOOK AT MY BODY AND ITS AGING, and I notice how time has affected me. My hair has grayed, and my face belongs to a man I hardly recognize—a man whose face has been hacked up by the years, a man with heavy eyes. My body, too, offers unpleasant reminders of the years gone by. My back tires easily, flabbiness has taken up residence around my middle, and an overall distrust of my plumbing pervades. I'm so different from the twenty-one-year-old who came into the prison system so long ago. The moxie and zip have transformed into quiet and soulful acceptance. Hell, even my phrases have aged.

Aging isn't just about time's effect on our bodies. It's also about the effect it has on our hearts and our ability to feel—to gather in everything we've seen, heard and experienced, and to somehow make sense of it all. To find *meaning* in that. If you find that in here, in prison, you're lucky.

I've been lucky enough to have met two guys in prison who've been my mentors in living, aging, and dying in prison. Huero and Mike didn't know it, but they were trainers for my soul. Their bare-knuckled bouts with pain and suffering taught me much. Though their luck ran out, they were the richest men in town. If you think in terms of money, well, this story ain't for you.

Huero was an old Mexican-white guy on the yard. I would see him out alone, feeding the assorted small birds, Brewer's blackbirds and sparrows. He gave them the leftover bread that is in abundance here. He had short gray hair and one eye. He was thin and slightly stoop-shouldered. But he was still fairly active, even coming out when it was warm to try his hand at slow-motion handball.

Two years earlier, a gal I was seeing suggested that it would be nice to get an older pen pal for her grandmother, Pearl, who was in her eighties. Her husband had passed away a few years before and she was lonely. I said I'd see what I could do, that I had somebody in mind.

The next time I saw Huero, I asked if he'd like to write to Pearl. I explained who she was and her desire for a pen pal. "Sure, why not?" he said.

They made an immediate connection, one that older people make with others their age that is both strange and wonderful.

After three months of writing to each other, Pearl came to visit him. Since my friend, Pearl's granddaughter, and I were visiting every weekend, we witnessed their first meeting.

Huero and Pearl greeted each other with grace and charm, then went off on their own to sit and talk. We watched them from a distant corner, hoping for the best, hoping for *something*. By the end of visiting, four hours later, they were acting like a couple of teenagers, smiling and gossiping. They even had secret inside jokes and glances. It was a marvel to watch.

They became the best of friends despite the setting and circumstances. Six months later, my lady friend told me some bad news: Pearl had been diagnosed with breast cancer. The doctor estimated that she had six months to live. I was sworn to secrecy. I also found out at this time via Pearl that Huero had been diagnosed with prostate cancer. He was refusing treatment and was also not expected to last long. I never asked him about it. I respected his privacy, as he was proud and reserved.

My friend moved and stopped visiting me, so I grew out of touch with what was going on with Huero and Pearl. Months went by. Then one day he stopped me on the yard. He told me that Pearl had passed away.

"I love and miss her very much," he said, staring off into the distant Sierra Nevada Mountains.

I watched his face, looking for it to break, but it didn't. His spoken sentiments, dry and gruff as they were, embodied a world of love and pain, joy and sorrow. A man of his age and generation held his cards tightly to his chest. What I'd seen was more than most ever saw.

I told him that I was sorry for his loss, that I knew he loved her. He thanked me, to the point of embarrassment, for bringing them together. She was the only true and pure thing in his life up until that time. We didn't talk about his illness. A man deserves his distance, his private suffering, in a way of his choosing. I gave him that.

Afterward, when I saw him out on the yard, feeding the birds or hitting a handball against the wall, still alone and to himself, I would sometimes say "Hi." But mostly I was silent, thankful for knowing one man's story—a peek into the thread of stories that stretch out and become a man's life.

Life is like that, isn't it? You get used to the routine, pass the days like all the rest, then—Bam! Fate or destiny throws an outside punch that lays you flat on your back. The Great Ones always get up, shake off the pain and continue.

I've known a few good fighters. But most people are like me, cowards through and through. We lay there on that mat, the roar of the crowd around us. We desperately search for a way out, a mother's skirt to hang on to, or we even surrender. Those were the kind of men I rubbed shoulders with, the kind of man I was.

Mike was a good-natured, older Mexican whom I knew until last year. That's when he died. One day he was among us, living in the same cell block a few houses away from me, then within a couple of months, he was diagnosed with cancer and rapidly wasted away and was gone.

I don't ever remember Mike being cross with anybody. He always had a smile and a "hello" handy. He was a guy you appreciated having around. His answer to stress or tough times was to grin and bear it, to knuckle down and work harder. The usual things everyone here bitches about—the food, the guards, the program—he never bothered to complain about. Oh, he would sympathize with the next guy, but senseless griping was not his way.

He told me that, on the streets, he had worked as a general laborer for many years, eventually working his way into the union. He gained a lot of experience from working the various jobs around construction sites. His skills and experience made him a valuable worker in prison. His prison job was one of the better paying—about ninety-five cents an hour, which is great in here, considering that just about all the jobs have been stripped of pay. So he did all right for himself out there on the streets, and in here. He was generous, too. If you asked him for something—even if you were simply hungry and wanted a soup or a bag of beans—he'd give it to you and tell you not to bother paying it back. But if he knew you were playing him, he'd tell you straight out, "I can't help you."

One day, he went out on a medical transport to a local hospital and ended up being gone for two weeks. People asked his cellmate where he was and if anything had happened to him, as he hadn't packed his property. It was strange for a guy to be out that long without any kind of word. Then, one day, the guards told his cellie to go ahead and pack his property. The guards didn't know anything and were only following orders. Rumors circulated. The only thing anybody knew for certain was that before he left, Mike had complained about stomach problems. Who knew what that was? Hell, most guys have some kind of indigestion problems. But Mike's absence became ominous.

I'll always remember when they brought him back. It was late at night, after count, and all the lights in the building were off. He was brought to his cell by a guard. He was thinner than I'd remembered, and slower. It then occurred to me that something was seriously wrong with him. When I had a chance to talk to Mike the next day, I found out exactly what.

He had been diagnosed with late-stage stomach cancer. He didn't have much chance of a recovery. His doctors were still going to treat him with chemotherapy. When he told me this, we both understood that it was futile, that it was more for effect than real hope. The smile he always had was trying to put in an appearance, but it was weak. The far-away look in his eyes betrayed him.

God, how I felt so naked and awkward, not knowing what to say or do. My impulse was to embrace him, to somehow convey that he was not alone in this world or in his suffering, that I—and everyone else, too—cared for him, that our sympathy would give him courage. But I didn't say anything close to that. My feelings were choked off in uncomfortable small talk. I told him, though, that if he needed anyone to talk to, he could come and talk to me. Then, I left.

After a week, when he had a chance to get around to talk to everyone, I spoke to him again. He seemed to be doing all right, at least getting some color back. He was ashen when he first returned, but now, with a little sun and fresh air, he looked better.

He was sitting out on the benches near the yard gate, waiting to be taken to the main infirmary. That's where the more serious medical cases were treated and where Mike would get his chemotherapy. I'd brought him a card that I had made and a few of the guys who knew him had signed wishing him well. That familiar smile of his greeted me.

"The doctor says that I have a good chance of recovery and it looks like the chemotherapy might knock it out and keep it from spreading," he told me. He made me believe, and I did. I wanted to.

The next time I saw Mike, I noticed something strange. As he sat out on the benches and waited for his treatment, he stood out a little more than usual, even though he sat there small and silent. I wondered to myself what it was that made me feel that way. Was it others' reactions toward him now that they knew he was dying? Was my own perception of him now altered? Or both?

Mike went to the outside hospital for two weeks. When he returned, he was thin and weak. His face was once again ashen. But the most noticeable thing about him now was his thousand-yard stare. *He knew.*

It was then that people kept their distance. It seemed that his wasting away and cancer had psychologically culled him from the herd. It was as though we had to accept that this happens for a reason; it's nature's way, and it's no use to worry or get sad. Life goes on.

If only I believed that.

While everyone else acted as if he were invisible, I felt myself inescapably drawn to him and intertwined in his fate. His life, and now his eventual death, had something to teach me, to give me. It was then that I went out of my way to help him as much as I could.

One day, I saw him sitting out on the benches for the longest time. He looked in bad shape and was in obvious pain. He had no business being out like that, and it angered me.

"Mike, how long have you been waiting out here?" I asked.

"They called me out three hours ago to go to the main infirmary," he told me, hunched over in resignation as the cold misty winter morning bit at him.

I looked around for an officer to explain Mike's situation to. Someone's gotta be able to help, I thought.

"Listen," I said. "Let's go over to the program office and try to get one of the cops to call on his radio and get you an escort." I helped him up, noticing that he'd lost a lot of mass from his frame. We walked over to a couple of officers who were watching the yard in front of the program office.

"Excuse me," I said, interrupting them. "My friend here has cancer and is in a lot of pain. He was called out to go to the main infirmary over three hours ago and has been waiting patiently. He shouldn't be suffering like this. Can you please call an escort to come over and get him?"

The guards continued to glance at the yard beyond us. "We'll see what we can do," one of them finally answered, reaching down to finger his radio.

I glanced at Mike to check his reaction. He was small and shivering. I squeezed his shoulder and told him that I'd see him later.

Mike went downhill from there. He was wasting away in front of all of us, dying slowly, in piecemeal fashion. And, with each pound lost, with each cancer cell born, it was as if God had carved out a chunk of our own hearts. How dare he, some thought; we do everything in our power *not* to feel, to be distracted and numb, and now this wastrel mocks us with his suffering.

The fact was that Mike gave everyone something, whether they wanted it or not. He gave them feeling. Some hid from that, and avoided it like the plague. Others shied away from it and felt uncomfortable in its presence, cast nervous glances at it, while others succumbed to it in sympathy. Me? I think I experienced them all. I abhorred him; I avoided him; I felt for him.

The last time I saw Mike was on a cold winter day. All the life had been sucked out of him; it was surprising that he was even able to still walk around. I walked up to him and said, "Good morning," even though I knew it wasn't. We sat there on the bench, out there in the mist and gloom, and we talked.

"You know," he began weakly, "it's funny how all the little things we occupy ourselves with are kinda insignificant when we're dying. I used to worry about whether a guy was going to pay me the money he owed or whether or not somebody disrespected me. Now, it seems so small, and I wonder why I ever worried myself about such things."

"Been there, done that," I told him. "I guess it's all about growing up and maturing." I looked at his hands and they were yellow and almost translucent. Gone were the strong brown ones.

"I stayed away from my daughter for years, believing that my ex had brainwashed her into hating me," he confided. "It wasn't true. I let that hate, hurt, and suspicion keep us apart. It kills me."

He swallowed hard, as if trying to swallow all the bitterness down into his gut where the cancer could kill it. I didn't say anything.

"If somebody would've asked me before if I was scared of death, I would've told them only a violent death. Or a poor and lonely one. I don't care so much about a natural death. Shit, we all owe nature a death. But a violent one? No thanks; I'll pass," he said, chuckling at his words. So did I.

"What are you going to miss?" I asked, guessing he was in a reflective mood.

"Not the drugs or the booze, that's for sure," he said, raising his voice. Then, quietly, he said, "I'll miss my family, my daughter, and all the opportunities I passed to do the right thing."

"You got friends who'll miss you, too," I told him.

"Yeah, like the California Department of Corrections and Rehabilitation, for cheating them out of their life sentence!" he joked.

We both laughed at that one.

And that was it. The yard was recalled, and we went our separate ways, back to our housing units. That was the last I ever saw of him. He died three days later.

Life went on as usual, too busy to ever have noticed Mike passing through.

My own story is unfinished. It is still being written. It has taken a while to find meaning in the suffering in my own life. To accept it. Lessons have always come slow to me. They've been known to simmer on my stove for decades.

But what I've come to realize is that suffering is just fertilizer for my soul, that it takes a lot of crap, a lot of suffering, to craft and mature a soul. It can't be done without it.

Ronald F. Day

A Relationship Worthwhile

"**D**O YOU YEARN TO TELL A STORY about a relationship you had while in prison?"

After I was asked this question in an email, I reflected on relationships I had with women during my incarceration. My answer was going to be an emphatic "No."

I did not "yearn" to tell a story about failure. I was married in prison and divorced in prison. Although there were some highs during my marriage to a woman I met three years before I was incarcerated, there were many more lows. I definitely applaud my ex-wife for having the resolve to maintain a relationship with me for more than five years. But like many prison marriages that have to endure significant challenges, it gradually dissolved.

There was another relationship that I thought was promising. It certainly had potential. But with me at the beginning of a long stint in prison, it was going to be an awfully long time before our relationship would have some semblance of normalcy. It, too, did not work out.

After reflecting on those failures, I thought long and hard about the one relationship I had in prison that was not only successful but also profoundly fulfilling.

Generally, when we think of relationships, we think of people. This relationship was different. It involved only one person: me. The relationship that I felt enthusiastic talking about is the relationship I developed with learning. The good thing about this relationship is that it created a win-win situation. There was no room for failure.

But before I talk about learning, I have to explain why I dropped out of high school, turned my back on learning, and gave the middle finger to the educational system. To be frank, I never felt particularly challenged in school. I did well enough through junior high school, but I was an average student. I didn't have any particular talent, so there was no reason to be noticed by a teacher. The most recognition that I recall receiving as a young student was for my penmanship.

The students who typically received attention had special talents or behavioral problems. It's hard to be average in any school system, but it was especially so in New York, which had so many layers of bureaucracy and had come to accept mediocrity from many of its students.

In his campaign for a third trip to Gracie Mansion, Mayor Bloomberg said in a commercial, "When I became mayor, a dysfunctional and inept school system was failing our kids." Fortunately for him, he didn't have to personally experience this ineptness.

By high school, I had run into serious complications and had completely lost interest in school. The gravitational pull and lure of the streets was far stronger than that of underpaid teachers and an apathetic school system. So I simply dropped out in my second year of the ninth grade. The person most devastated by my decision to quit was my mother. She at first had no inkling that I was leaving home for school but ending up at my cousin's apartment, either sleeping or watching soap operas, or out on the street with my friends engaging in criminal activities.

Within a few months of abandoning school at fifteen, furthering my education had fallen completely off my radar. But as fate would have it, I had a cousin who dropped out in the eleventh grade and enrolled in a GED program. She asked me if I was interested in these classes. I told her that I was absolutely uninterested; I knew that in our neighborhood, even people who stayed in school were still struggling. But my cousin went off to school each night, studied, and prepared to take the GED test. On the day of the test, she asked me if I wanted to take it, too. I had not studied one day for the exam and wasn't even sure that I'd be able to take it. She assured me that I could, since she had put my name on the roster. I thought, what the heck, I could get away from the block for a few hours.

Sure enough, we arrived at the testing site and my name was on the list. Along with dozens of other students, I sat down and took the exam. It certainly wasn't easy. I racked my brain over many of the math and science problems and was relieved when it was over. I thought I did reasonably well, considering the circumstances, but probably not well enough to pass. My cousin was more confident than me. A few weeks later we received our test results in the mail. I had passed; she failed.

When my mother found out that I passed the test, she sat me down and said, "Son, you have a good head on your shoulders. You don't have to end up like so many other young black men out there. You can go to college." It was 1986. I was seventeen years old. What she told me went in one ear and out the other. The idea of going to college never resonated.

I thought I had all the answers. I was a drug dealer, and my dealing had intensified. I was deeply engrossed in the lifestyle. Like most people, I didn't consider the long-term consequences of my actions. I lived for the moment, for instant gratification. I wanted to make some fast money and reap the rewards of bucking the system.

This type of tunnel vision clearly has ramifications. Within a few years, I had been arrested several times. Some of my friends had been murdered, others had been sentenced to lengthy prison terms, and some had become addicted to drugs. I later learned that, as the popular quotation goes, "Insanity is doing the same thing over and over again and expecting a different result." It didn't take long for my time to come. So despite having leadership and organizational skills and other strong qualities, I was in the wrong line of work.

For devaluing and demoralizing my community and putting people's lives at risk, I had to pay a stiff penalty: fifteen to forty-five years in state prison.

Unfortunately, I—and many other young black men from my neighborhood and other poor communities—had come to accept incarceration as inevitable. About as many of us had gone to prison as had graduated from high school. We were prepared, at least externally, for this predicament. Some of us had even insanely welcomed it as a "badge of honor."

Do the Time: Don't Let the Time Do You

I had been locked up for a little over a year before I was transferred to Sing Sing Correctional Facility. I noticed almost immediately that some men in the population were taking advantage of the opportunity to attend college. While this had been an option for some of them before prison, clearly it had not been a priority. There are simply far too many distractions in the street.

Being *captive* is different. It's clearly a constraint, but it can provide opportunity for people who are open to change. As Malcolm X once said, "I'd put prison second to college as the best place for a man to go if he needs to do some thinking. If he's motivated, in prison he can change his life." So I enrolled in Mercy College, and despite the rigmarole of life in prison, I did pretty well the first semester. Since Mercy is a four-year college and Sing Sing also has a program that offers a master's degree, I started thinking long-term. This was the first time that I had really considered earning a college degree. In this abyss of hopelessness and uncertainty, the future did not seem so bleak.

After that first semester of studies at Sing Sing, I was transferred to Green Haven Prison. At Green Haven, I enrolled in Dutchess Community College and was three classes shy of an associate's degree when the funding for college prison programs was cut. I was utterly disheartened. I had embarked on a journey that I hoped would lead to a college degree. I wanted to do things differently post-incarceration. I believed that an education would help me, particularly since people who earn degrees while in prison are far less likely to recidivate. But notwithstanding all the data on the huge benefits of college prison programs, the rug had been abruptly snatched out from under me and many others.

Although the opportunity to earn a formal education had all but disappeared, I was determined not to give up on the learning process. I frequented the facility's law library on a regular basis. The law began to interest me so much that I enrolled in a legal research course and eventually began working in the law library. Becoming intimate with crime had resulted in my imprisonment, so I hoped that becoming intimate with the law would result in my release. Learning about the law didn't get me out of prison, but it became a way for me to understand on a deeper level how my crimes and the crimes of those around me impacted society.

As my comprehension of the law increased, so did my ability to articulate complex legal issues. What I found particularly striking was that so many bright men, some of them with the knowledge and depth of the law that would make them brilliant attorneys, had instead committed themselves to violating the law. I was one of these people.

Besides working in the law library, I became involved in a program called Partnership for a Calculated Transition (PACT). This group held biweekly legal seminars with Yale law students during the fall and spring semesters. This interaction also increased my understanding of the criminal justice system and the judicial process. I felt privileged, despite the venue, to interact with law students who would become prominent lawyers, judges, CEOs, and legislators. For their part, the law students would routinely talk about how they benefited from hearing our stories and recommendations for criminal justice reform.

I also became a member of the National Trust for the Development of African-American Men (the Trust), participating in leadership development training and becoming familiar with the Trust philosophy, including that all human behavior is driven by values. In our training, Dr. Garry A. Mendez, Jr., the executive director of the Trust, told us this: "I can't get you out of prison, but I can help you become assets to your community."

Before this, I had not really connected my crimes to my value system. It may sound naïve that it took my going to prison to make this connection, but I had simply not done much deep thinking about how my behavior impacted society. The Trust helped me to do this, and to develop a *sense of community*. Furthermore, I learned from the Trust that I have a *civic duty* to give back to the community—and this duty required me to start with the *community* behind bars.

I was ultimately transferred to several other prisons and became involved in myriad programs. I became a facilitator for Aggression Replacement Training (ART), a peer counselor for the Transitional Services Center, a peer educator for Prisoners for AIDS Counseling and Education (PACE), and then the director of the PACE program at Fishkill Correctional Facility. I wrote articles that were published in national AIDS publications, and a play about tattooing in prison that was turned into a DVD *(Lasting Impressions)*.

To some extent, it seemed like a lifetime, but fifteen years had finally crept by. It was time for me to appear before the parole board. I had been preparing for my release by transforming my life, and now I would be judged. I had done mock parole board hearings and gotten ready for what I knew would be an uphill battle. Although I felt good about my prospects, I was still in prison for a violent offense. And plenty of people around me were being denied parole, often repeatedly.

But I went before a parole panel that was sympathetic. The two commissioners listened to my story, asked probing questions, and gave me some valuable insight. I actually left the hearing feeling optimistic. Two days later a sergeant handed me the envelope. Friends and associates gave me space but eyed me from a distance, trying to read my reaction.

I opened the envelope and scrolled down to the bottom of the page: "Request for parole granted. Open date August 29, 2007."

It's difficult to describe how I felt inside, but I let out a resounding "Yes!" and had the biggest smile I could ever muster. I was ecstatic, especially considering that I could have been denied parole at least eight times, or until my conditional release date fifteen years later. That night tears welled up in my eyes as the thought of finally being released from prison began to sink in.

Continued Success

I wanted my relationship with learning to continue after my release from prison. Consequently, I went to multiple college open houses and visited dozens of college web sites. I eventually settled on Empire State College. I chose Empire because it's affordable, has flexible programs, and a willingness to provide credit for life experience. Programs at Empire usually involve intensive writing, but this didn't pose a problem for me. I was simply delighted to be working towards one of my academic goals.

I transferred in approximately sixty credits to Empire, earned additional credits for College Level Examination Program (CLEP) exams and life experience, took three semesters of classes, and completed my studies in June 2007.

My mentor at Empire was impressed enough with me that she recommended that the college write an article about me for its web site or its newsletter. Sure enough, I was contacted by the main campus and worked with a communications representative to write a compelling story about my educational journey. The college also asked me to interview for a new part-time position as an alumni peer coach. My name had surfaced because my mentor believed that I would be a good candidate for the job. Because so many black male college students are dropping out, Empire received a grant to hire two alumni peer coaches to help such students navigate the system, continue their studies, and succeed in college.

Approximately two weeks after I was interviewed, I received a call from the interviewer. "If you're still interested in the position, we'd love to have you," he said.

While I was wrapping up my studies at Empire, I was also applying to graduate school. Unlike the many people who take a break after graduating from college, I determined that I had had enough break time in prison. I found myself scrambling for reference letters, assessing programs, trying to meet application deadlines, all while maintaining good grades. I seriously considered (and ruled out) master's degrees in social work and public health, both excellent options. I decided instead to pursue a master's degree in public administration (MPA). I felt this was most consistent with the nonprofit leadership track that I'm interested in.

I applied to three CUNY (City University of New York) schools with MPA programs: John Jay, City College, and Baruch, which was definitely my preference. Less than a month after turning in my application, I received a letter from Baruch's Director of Student Affairs and Graduate Admissions. The first paragraph said, "On behalf of the faculty of the School of Public Affairs, I am pleased to offer you acceptance into the MPA program for the fall 2009 semester. This decision reflects our recognition of your particular talents and strong academic record, and our wish for you to join our exciting graduate community."

I was absolutely thrilled.

My main concern at this juncture was whether or not I could work while attending graduate school. I knew that this wouldn't be easy, but I believed that "where there's a will there's a way." Working for Empire would provide me with a great opportunity to encourage black men, both young and old, to hang in there until they accomplish the goal of earning college degrees.

Through it all, I learned something very fundamental about my relationship with learning: If I had developed this relationship many years ago, there's a good chance that I would not have ended up entangled in the criminal justice system. One of my critical decisions, which preceded my decision to engage in a criminal lifestyle, was to drop out of school. Had I been as focused and as interested in earning a quality education then as I am now, the sky would have been the limit.

As a formerly incarcerated person, I now have serious constraints and limitations. And I have no one to blame but myself. I chose what I thought was the path of least resistance, and it ended up being a dead-end street.

My relationship with learning will never put me in a position to right my wrongs. It has, however, enabled me to do some critical thinking about my life. Indeed, I have come to the realization that despite my past, I will make significant strides as long as I apply myself and remain steadfast in pursuit of realistic goals. It has also put me in a position to help others who are interested in developing a similar relationship.

In addition to working at Empire as a peer coach, I am now a senior career coach for the Osborne Association, a criminal justice organization. In that capacity, I have encouraged dozens of men and women to continue their education. I have found that many people without a high school diploma or GED want to earn one, and those with a diploma are interested in continuing their education.

However, there is a disconnect between what the vast majority of people want and what they actually pursue. Left to their own devices, many people will not return to school, despite knowing that they increase their earning power with each diploma they receive. People tell me all the time that they don't want to get stuck in entry-level positions. "So what are you doing to prevent this from happening?" I ask. Most respond that they want to go to school or obtain some additional training, but few have a plan to do so.

What's important is that these individuals want to work, instead of "throwing bricks at the penitentiary." They would rather make entry-level money than expose themselves to continued arrest, incarceration, and shame. But the challenge is getting people motivated enough to actually pursue the education they say they want. Too many people think they can't pass the GED test or earn a degree. Some have been out of school so long that they fret about returning. Others claim that the priority is a job. But once they secure a job, the GED or degree is put on the backburner.

In this context, I think the single most important thing I can do is act as a role model. I routinely tell people, "If I can do it, then so can you." I also tell them about the steps I took and encourage them to do the same. One thing I refrain from doing, however, is letting people get away with lame excuses.

Indeed, I'll ask a man or woman recently released from prison whether he or she has a high school diploma or GED. Far too often the answer is "No." "Why don't you have one?" I ask. Typical responses include: "I didn't find time to do it." "Education wasn't important to the administration." Or, "I was focusing on my case."

Barring a learning disability, there is little reason that a person should be released from prison, especially after serving long-term incarceration, without a GED. Unfortunately, too many people are simply unmotivated, unchallenged, and apathetic about continuing their education. My hope is that these individuals will look within to find the courage and determination to challenge themselves, and develop a relationship with learning.

It will be a relationship worthwhile. It certainly has been for me.

Sheila R. Rule

A Matter of Time

I WAS SURE THAT I'D MADE MY PEACE with time. And then I fell in love with a younger man who was doing time.

Before I met him, my forties had brokered a truce between time and me. That was the decade of my life where time suddenly loomed large and menacing in the form of a mid-life crisis. It chased me down, threw me against a wall, and made me pay respect to its fleet-footedness, made me think that I was running out of it. Time forced me to turn a steady gaze on my own reflection. Looking back at me was a woman who was living big dreams as a foreign correspondent for a prestigious newspaper, traveling the world, chronicling unfolding history. But the sadness in the reflection revealed to me that those dreams were better suited for someone else. They were not my own.

So, I dusted off my stored-up dreams and made them come true. I adopted a bright and gregarious three-year-old boy and made him mine. I bought an apartment in a good building and a good neighborhood and made it home. I developed a community of friends. I planted roots deep. Time settled into a quiet little corner of my life. I knew it was running—it left gray hair and faint facial lines as annoying reminders—but for the most part, it honored our agreement: It didn't bother me, and I didn't bother it.

Then I met Joe. And time went back on its word.

It happened just as I was getting acquainted with my fifties, and settling into my hard-won satisfaction. I didn't have a man in my life, but I wasn't suffering from the lack of one. I'd had my fair share of love, romance, and marriage through the years, and I had finally arrived at a place in life where having a man—or not—did not define me, did not rule my sense of who I was. If a man came along, it would be my pleasure to explore love's possibilities again, but I no longer felt that I *needed* a man to make me whole.

What I felt I *needed* was to be of service, to show my gratitude for all of my blessings by giving back. I'd done a range of volunteer work over the years—from working with girls in a group home to helping the homeless make the transition to permanent housing—and was ready to again spread my wings in that direction. I stumbled upon what I was looking for one Sunday after services at Riverside Church in Manhattan. At an event designed to attract new members, the congregation's many clubs and organizations were displaying brochures and offering goodies.

At one table sat a representative of the church's prison ministry. I talked to her about the ministry's work on behalf of the incarcerated and formerly incarcerated. I wondered if there was something I could do to help, especially since so many of those in prison are African-American, like me. I started attending monthly meetings and was soon handed a few letters that the ministry had received in the last few months from people in prison. I was asked to write back.

I responded to the letters, and to the scores upon scores of letters that followed. I always signed my letters the same: "Keep the faith, Sheila." I'd been told by prison ministry leaders that including last names and other personal information was not required nor advised.

I looked forward to stopping by the prison ministry mailbox after Sunday services and scooping up all of the envelopes addressed to "Sheila, Riverside Church Prison Ministry." Letter after letter allowed me the privilege of putting human faces, sharp minds, and longing hearts to the statistics and stereotypes to which these men and women had been reduced.

In the mailbox one Sunday was a short letter from a Joe Robinson, incarcerated in a prison at the foot of the Catskill Mountains. He started his letter by saying that although he was in prison, "my soul is free." He added that he was looking for a "young woman" with whom to correspond.

Well-versed by then in the ways of the prison ministry—we didn't do love connections and, besides, everyone in the prison ministry was middle-age and beyond—I gently responded that we did not have any "young women" for him to write to, but that with a soul such as his, I had no doubt that he would find what he was searching for. I dropped the letter in the mail and moved on to other things.

It wasn't long before another letter from Joe appeared in the mailbox. This one, unblinkingly direct, explained that the phrase "young woman" was simply a turn of phrase. That said, he did want to correspond with a woman, in the hope of developing a relationship that might lead to something more. And then Joe etched with his words a self-portrait: a thirty-two-year-old man who took full responsibility for his crime; a man who by the strength of his very own will had transformed his thinking and his life; the father of a boy stepping into his teens; a self-confident doer and a dreamer who wanted to do well for himself and his family by doing good and giving back to others; a man who still held onto his boyhood dreams of becoming a pilot someday, just like his long-absent father.

What I most remember now about that letter is not its exact contents, but how honestly and powerfully it was written—and how powerfully it affected me. What a good human being, I thought. I responded as honestly and directly as he had written to me. I told him that the prison ministry could not help him find a companion, and that I certainly could not fill that role. But I told him that I could be his friend, as I was to other incarcerated men and women with whom I corresponded.

That's how our friendship began. We wrote back and forth for more than a year, with each letter filling in more and more blanks about Sheila and Joe—who we'd been and who we hoped to become. And with each letter, we grew closer.

Yet, I refused to acknowledge—to Joe or myself—that my feelings for him were growing, deepening, taking my heart in unexpected and unwanted directions. I had no qualms about loving a man in prison, especially an uncommon man like Joe. The problem for me was that Joe was twenty years younger. While I applauded and even admired other women who loved younger men, a huge gap in age wasn't for me. I never really thought about why. I just felt it in my gut.

But all the while, I was slowly and certainly dropping my guard with Joe. "Sheila of the Prison Ministry" revealed her real last name. I gave him my address at work—my home address was still off-limits—so that I could receive and respond to his letters more promptly. I allowed him to call me collect, so that we could have real conversations. As for Joe, his letters grew heavy with intimations of love and affection for me but, ever respectful, he never gave full voice to the words in his heart.

As the months went by, I started feeling the timelessness of love. I started feeling that Joe and I were unaffected by time. We were ageless. And there was the sensation of being weightless, too. The sensation of floating above the clouds, unencumbered. No one there but us.

In the thirteenth month of our correspondence, I agreed to do something Joe had asked me to do earlier in our friendship: visit him. I'd declined before, concerned that meeting face to face might disrupt our blossoming friendship, might throw unexpected, unwanted emotions in the mix. Joe had sent me a photo of his sweet face; I had not sent a photo in return. But by that thirteenth month, my heart had a mind of its own.

So one weekday morning in the autumn of 2003, I traveled to the prison where Joe lived and sat across from him at a small wooden table in a nearly empty visiting room. We talked like old friends, and hugged each other like brother and sister when it was time for me to go.

Less than a month later, as if in a trance, I sat down at my computer, typed out this letter, and mailed it to him:

Joe:

If I do not say this, I will explode...

I love you. I love you.

I am in love with you. I am in love with you. I am in love with you. I am in love with you. I am in love with you. I am in love with you. I am in love with you. I am in love with you. I am in love with you. I am in love with you. I am in love with you. I am in love with you. I am in love with you. I am in love with you.

I love you, Joe. I am in love with you, Joe.

To be continued...

Joe wrote back, and on the outside of the envelope were these words: "I love you, too." We were married about a year later in the prison visiting room where we'd first met face to face.

After five years of marriage and our share of burdens, Joe and our love can still make me float, still give me that feeling of weightlessness. This is the best relationship I have ever had.

It fills me up and brings me joy like no other. I have grown as a human being in ways that I could not have imagined.

But feeling the timelessness of it all is a harder thing. After I fell in love with Joe, time awoke from its hibernation and left that quiet little corner of my life. Once again, it started looming large.

More than anything, time taunts us with its stinginess. There is never enough of it. Even though we know that we are blessed to have the time we are given, there is still never enough.

Visiting hours at Joe's prison are from 9:00 a.m. to 3:00 p.m. I try to show up as close to 9:00 as possible, so that we can have the benefit of the full six hours. But far too soon, we hear the prison guard announce, "The visiting room is now closed. Please say your goodbyes at the table." Joe and I stand, embrace and part. I turn and blow him a kiss. He waves back. I walk through the door and head home. He lines up with other men at the back of the room and heads back to his cell.

Our phone calls are exactly thirty minutes long. At twenty-nine minutes, a disembodied, take-charge voice elbows in to say that we have one minute left. The voice interrupts again when there are thirty seconds left. If there's no line of men waiting for the phone, Joe sometimes calls back. That second time, when the thirty-second announcement comes, we say a hurried "I love you" and hang up. There've been a few occasions when we weren't quick enough, with the phone call ending unceremoniously and the "I love you" chopped off.

The other day, I received from the prison a copy of a form that was sent to Joe with these instructions: "We will start processing visitors at 12:00 p.m. on February 16. Your visit will end at 8:00 a.m. on February 18. Your visitors must arrive on time (12:00 noon). If they will be late, they 'MUST' contact us prior to 10:00 a.m. on the date of the FRP visit. NO VISITORS WILL BE PROCESSED AFTER 2:00 p.m."

FRP stands for Family Reunion Program, commonly known by the families that participate as "trailers." Joe and I are allowed to go on a trailer about every three months. For forty-four hours, we find what passes for normal in the confines of a homey little two-bedroom trailer on the grounds of the prison. We play house. We love hard. We watch our favorite news programs and favorite entertainment. We dance. We cook. We laugh. We talk, talk, talk. We behave like what we are—two people who have a strong and loving marriage. We almost lose ourselves, but not quite—at 6:45 a.m., 11:40 a.m., 4:45 p.m. and 10:45 p.m., Joe has to stop whatever he's doing and stand outside the trailer's front door for "the count" of all incarcerated men in the facility. And in the fortieth or forty-first hour, I often find myself lying awake, thinking that there's never enough time.

I sometimes wonder if there'll ever be enough time. I am on a forced march toward my sixtieth birthday, and I'm finding that time is getting stingier still. Although I thought I was running out of it in my forties, I know that I am running out of it now. And it offers absolutely no provisions for replenishment. I'm running out of time to experience all of the plans, to realize all of the dreams, to go all of the places, and see all of the things that Joe and I talk about. I'm running out of time to live life with Joe on the outside, in real time—not as we do now, storing up our thoughts, ideas and concerns, storing up our joy and anger, storing up our desire to be held and our need to be comforted—storing all of that up until Joe can make a collect call or I can drive up for a visit.

Joe has about six years to go on a twenty-five-to-life sentence, the result of a barroom confrontation that tragically ended in the loss of a man's life. I find myself constantly wishing, praying that Joe is released early. He has transformed his life; he is more than ready to come home. He is more than ready to live a life that will honor his potential, as well as the potential of the young man who died on that barroom floor. But if Joe must serve all six of those remaining years, my wish, my prayer is that they pass in a blinding flash.

Every now and then when I say that prayer, time rears its menacing head again and leaves me with this thought: When you're heading toward sixty, wishing years away is wishing your life away. When you're staring at sixty, you try to harness years. You try to make them stand still. You don't wish them away. Not when you're heading toward sixty.

So, all these years after my truce with time, it is waging war again. But I'm determined that I will not go down without a fight. I will defiantly continue to wish and pray that the years pass in that blinding flash, until Joe is home. If that's wishing my life away, so be it.

For what I know is this: When Joe comes home, no matter how many years are left, I will have the time of my life.

CONTRIBUTORS

In addition to offering biographical information, the authors express their hopes and dreams for themselves and humanity, as well as gratitude to the special people in their lives.

Safiya E. Bandele

I consider myself blessed, having been raised in small-town Wilson, North Carolina, experiencing a childhood saturated with black southern culture, rich in lore, values, and memories. I graduated from the segregated Charles H. Darden High School and, in 1969, from historically black Johnson C. Smith University. I moved to Brooklyn that same year, reuniting with my mother, my maternal aunts, and my daughter, who was born in my junior year in high school. In May 1969, I met ibn Kenyatta. He was arrested January 1974, convicted and sentenced for "attempted murder of a policeman." I worked on his defense/offense committee.

I am committed to traveling this path with him—with love, perseverance, and loyalty. I am nearing retirement after thirty-three years of service to Medgar Evers College of The City University of New York—as professor and administrator of the college's Center for Women's Development. Just as I consider my childhood a blessing, I thank God, too, for the richly rewarding decades of experience and opportunities to learn from "challenges" at Medgar Evers and the central Brooklyn community where I continue to reside, and for the complicated, joyous, sometimes hurtful three decades—doing the bid with Kenyatta.

Kenneth R. Brydon

Walking in faith, I see that my life is best suited to trust in God for outcomes. With thirty-one years now served, life is surprisingly busy. Divorced and in my early fifties, I'm currently organizing a National Prison Writing Contest for Christians, and a Christian creative writing program here at San Quentin Prison that will help to continue to improve the writing skills of prisoners (myself included). I'd like to acknowledge the San Quentin Brothers in Pen Creative Writing Class and certainly our wonderful instructor, Zoe Mullery, for her own sacrifices in making the class and three anthologies *(http://brothersinpen. wordpress.com)* happen. Further appreciation is extended to the Prison University Project, which gave me the degree that pointed me to my love of words.

Stacy L. Burnett

I hail from the majestic Hudson River Valley and traveled extensively until corralled at Albion Correctional Facility in New York. I've been working on overcoming my "middle-child syndrome" while incarcerated and plan to take my son kayaking to see Antarctica's penguins as soon as my future parole officer grants me permission to leave the state—in five to ten years. I've written under several pen names but no longer care to hide anything I've said or done or worry about others' responses. As Sarah Harrington, I self-published *My Dad the Lesbian* and sold almost 4,500 copies. As the title suggests, my father now lives as a woman. While I was in county jail, my mother died of a rare cancer called carcinoid syndrome. I strongly urge everyone with a diagnosis of irritable bowel syndrome diagnosis to be screened for carcinoid cancer.

I will always be madly in love with my son's father—he is brilliant and adorable and as much a free spirit as I am. He is a remarkable father and I am proud my son is a receptacle for his DNA. Aaah, yes—my son. All of my tomorrows belong to him. The entire Dupont/Distasi/Mackey clan has my undying gratitude for all the love they pour into our little boy. Before I die, I hope to be worthy of his affection. Anyone interested can write me: c/o Kathy Dupont, P.O. Box 1342, Highland, NY, 12528, or to Stacy L. Burnett, #09G0379, Albion Correctional Facility, 3595 State School Road, Albion, New York 14411-9399.

Jason Dansby

I am a native North Carolinian—from Asheville, to be exact! My greatest accomplishments are my children. My main goal is that after I have been called to the Lord, my children look back over my life and view me as a success. I have three biological children—Dejaun, five; Ricardo, three; and Zacharie, two—and three stepchildren. I hope the future brings them the same great opportunities I have been blessed with. The fact that our president is half-black and half-white has shown my children and me that there are no more excuses for not doing something with our lives. My greatest hope for my future is to be looked at as a person who, despite having done wrong, has decided to rise above the proverbial shackles linking me to a past of nothingness. I would like the readers of *The Think Outside the Cell Series* to read my stories and know that just because you have hit rock bottom doesn't mean you cannot dust yourself off and climb to the top. Some people might prejudge you, but the most important people will judge you by the content of your character, not by the content of your rap sheet.

Ronald F. Day

I was born in Harlem and raised in the Bronx, New York. In 2011, I will earn my master's of public administration with a specialization in nonprofit administration from Baruch College. My goal is to earn a doctoral degree in criminal justice. I currently work as a senior career coach in workforce development for the Osborne Association.

My hope for the future is that as a society we will become less reliant on incarceration and become more reliant on education, especially for those who live in marginalized and underserved communities. I now believe, as Malcolm X said,

"Education is your passport to the future, for tomorrow belongs to the people who prepare for it today."

Darrin Goldberg

I have accomplished what so many of my dearly departed friends and associates have not: an opportunity to make it out of my adolescence and young-adult years, and to fully develop into a mature, spiritually conscious man. I have chosen to spend the last thirteen-and-one-half years in prison—over one-third of my thirty-seven years of life—elevating my consciousness and further educating myself. In fact, it is fair to say that in prison I have learned far more about myself, my intellectual capacity, and my responsibilities to humanity than I did in grade school, high school, and college. With the accumulation of learning, and a newfound awe of freedom and social equity, I plan to engage in several efforts geared toward helping young adults and children avoid falling victim to the self-destructive path that ultimately leads to imprisonment. I have spent the better part of the past thirteen-and-one-half years serving my community in this manner, and I hope to continue these efforts after my July 1, 2010 release, through speaking engagements, music production, and the publica-tion of several literary works that I wrote with these essential ends in mind.

Scott Gutches

I was born in 1970 and have moved frequently throughout northern New Jersey. Although I graduated from high school in Fair Lawn, if I were to claim any place as my "hometown," it would be Prospect Park, the Jersey town where I spent my formative years. However, I wouldn't be writing today if it weren't for Elenore Brangan, my eleventh- and twelfth-grade English teacher at Fair Lawn, under whom I learned to love to read and subsequently, although feebly, aspired to write. My brother, Paul, also deserves credit for not giving up and refusing to enable me through the usual family legacy of superficial endorsements while accepting lame excuses. Above all, I have to give Karen credit for tipping me in the right direction; without her, it is doubtful I could have ever survived, let alone rebuilt. Karen, I love you!

I am currently involved in a creative writing workshop sponsored by Jim Ciletti, an award-winning poet who tirelessly dedicates one afternoon a week to support us. It is in this community that my writing has flourished—thanks, guys! We are collaborating on establishing our own literary magazine, accepting pieces from staff and inmates alike. I am working on a memoir titled *Brooms in the Closet, Rugs in the Kitchen*. And with the help of Karen and Paul, I maintain my writing at *http://gutreaxshun.blogspot.com*.

Tanea Lunsford

I am a San Francisco native and a student at Columbia University in New York. My father has been incarcerated periodically throughout my entire life, which has been my motivation for pursuing a higher education and breaking the cycle of incarceration in my family. I have dreams of becoming a medical doctor and traveling the world. Writing is my passion, though my main goal in life is to be a resource to anyone in need.

Vickie Nelson

I love writing. We learn in school that reading can take you all over the world; I actually believe that writing offers that same experience—only better. Writing is liberating for me, and I truly thank God for my "pen." I have a passion for equal rights for women and girls, and I teach self-love and self-respect as a prerequisite to a successful life. Women, as the weaker sex by divine design, are discriminated against and disrespected in unimaginable ways, and this must change. So, I have started an organization called the Mae Esther Foundation, through which I hope to usher girls and young women into a new way of thinking, doing, and loving themselves tremendously. Then when people meet them, respect would be absolutely automatic. I've heard it said that at forty, women really start to live dynamic lives. Based on my life, there has never been a truer statement.

Randy Peters

I loved writing in high school but because of financial problems had to give it up and go to work. A little over twenty years later, I had the chance to pick it up again and have been running with it ever since. I've been writing seriously for about two-and-a-half years now. I've had several pieces published locally and completed a novel about a wolf pack pushed out of its home and forced to flee after killing a farmer. I am currently working on a novel about a northern Vermont boy growing up amidst alcoholism and abuse. I continue to write short stories and poetry, hoping for placement in ever larger publications. My wife, Donna, is my largest source of support. She has always been there for me, through good times and bad. I owe all my success to her unwavering love and devotion. The Community High School of Vermont has helped me with technical aspects of my writing, reference books, and computer access.

Marlon Peterson

I am a first-generation American of Trinidadian heritage. Born and raised in Crown Heights, Brooklyn, New York, I maximized my ten-year "sabbatical" in prison. I transformed my prison experience into a university of learning. With the support of my family and community of friends, I have used my gifts and talents to help those inside and outside the walls. I am a writer, educator, counselor, public speaker, and a man with a beautiful mind. I intend to continue working toward a degree in criminal justice, and to give a voice to the voiceless. To read more of my writing, go to *http://pensfromthepen1.blogspot.com.*

Lise Porter

I grew up in San Diego. I work as a licensed marriage and family therapist in an eating disorder program, and have worked with ex-felons, the elderly, children and teens, Vietnam vets, and the chronically mentally ill. I have a theater background and incorporate theater techniques into my work. I love to write and aspire to be a professional author, writing on issues of spirituality and healing. My current writing includes a feature-length screenplay, *Twenty Words for Snow*. I will be taking classes in the Master of Divinity program at Fuller Theological Seminary—and hope to continue some of my hobbies, which include swimming, yoga, and dance.

Frank Reid

I am from Richmond, Virginia. I've been in prison since I was twenty, about ten years. Through the experience of imprisonment, I've come to appreciate life in a substantially new way. These past ten years have so radically altered me as a person, as a human being, that I'm now dedicated to bringing about a political, social and economic order that appreciates human life in a fundamentally different way. Plainly put, I'm a revolutionary. More than that, I am a human being who desires to live in a world without poverty, hunger, homelessness, illiteracy, and racism. I'm ready to live without sexism and homophobia. Spare me the suffering and insanity of war. I need pollution-free and contaminant-free air, soil, and water to continue to exist on this planet. I want to live without oppression and injustice. It is my belief that, unless humanity rises up and embraces a moral consciousness that is wholly consistent with our potential as the highest form of intelligence on the planet, we will continue to bear the misery and pain of unnecessary death and destruction all over the world. Our lives will continue to be dominated by the impulsive cruelties of our own and other people's most base desires. A qualitatively better life is within our collective reach. Embrace your humanity.

Corey John Richardson

I am a former clinician, with a master's degree in Physician Assistant Studies from the University of Nebraska's College of Medicine in Omaha. I also have a bachelor's degree in Health Science/Physician Assistant Certificate from the University of Florida's College of Public Health. I hold an MBA from Salve Regina University's Graduate Business School in Newport, Rhode Island, and have completed doctoral health science coursework with a focus on prison health care at Spalding University in Louisville, Kentucky. My work has been incorporated into criminology courses at the University of Cincinnati and has been included in a congressional file on correctional health care in support of HR 3710. As a *pro se* litigant, I won a precedent-setting case on appeal against the Kentucky Department of Corrections regarding abuse of power (Richardson v. Rees, 283 S.W. 3d 257). I have also worked as a facilitator in numerous psychotherapeutic and recovery programs. I have written extensively about prison issues and sobriety, and several of my essays have been published in the book *Voices Through the Wall*. I maintain a web site at *http://coreyrichardson.blogspot.com*.

Joseph Robinson

I've been teaching personal finance and entrepreneurship to incarcerated men since 1995. I'm a certified instructor of Inmates Teaching Entrepreneurship and Mentoring (ITEM), a program I founded with Steve Mariotti, president and founder of the Network for Teaching Entrepreneurship (NFTE).

ITEM trains the incarcerated to teach their children and fellow incarcerated persons the basics of business ownership. I tapped into the power of my own entrepreneurial gifts after I was imprisoned in 1992 for a crime related to an illegal drug business I operated. My appetite for legitimate business was whetted as I read the business pages of newspapers that other prisoners discarded. I built my own business library by trading cigarettes for books, and I eventually became the go-to person for fellow incarcerated men seeking information about entrepreneurship. But missing from my library was a book on entrepreneurship written specifically for the incarcerated. I knew that if I wanted to read one, I would have to write it. The result is the well-received *Think Outside the Cell: An Entrepreneur's Guide for the Incarcerated and Formerly Incarcerated* (2007, Resilience Multimedia). I am married to Sheila R. Rule; we have two sons, Sean and Joseph.

Sheila R. Rule

I am founder and president of Resilience Multimedia, a publishing company that reflects my passion for social justice. My first contribution was a self-help book called *Think Outside the Cell: An Entrepreneur's Guide for the Incarcerated and Formerly Incarcerated,* by Joseph Robinson, my husband. I received a grant from the Ford Foundation to produce my next project, a series of books—including this one—designed to present a fairer, more balanced image of the incarcerated, the formerly incarcerated, and their loved ones. Before becoming a publisher, I was a journalist at *The New York Times* for more than thirty years. My beats included the New York State Legislature, social services, the homeless, civil rights, and pop music. I was also a foreign correspondent in Africa and Europe. I was a senior editor when I retired from *The Times* in order to fully embrace publishing. Joe and I have a striving, working marriage and two sons, Sean and Joseph.

Preston Seville

I am from Harlem and a May Taurus of Sicilian, Yorubian, Indian, and Boriqua descent. Some friends say I am a "mutt ☺," but I'd prefer to classify myself as a melting pot of diversity. I love to live and live to write. Writing has provided me with an outlet and a release for my experiences, expressions, and frustrations. Regardless of my circumstances, I aspire to be better and to do better for myself and those around me. I believe that all people should be treated equally. Outside of my passion for writing poetry and short stories, I am pursuing my bachelor's degree in human services. I love boxing (sparring and training), cooking (particularly seafood and pasta), and natural or landscaped sceneries. I have accomplished so much in my life. In the future I intend to run a program for troubled, at-risk teens. I thank everyone for reading my story. I hope that you glean wisdom from my pain. Keep the faith.

Daniel Skalla

I'm from Davenport, Iowa. I have been free for some months now and am enjoying life. I am a typical Iowan. I enjoy working hard and spending my time outside. I love playing with my kids.

I made many wrong choices in my past and spent most of life empty and unfulfilled. I had someone ask me to accept Christ and I did, but I continued to struggle with drugs and alcohol. Eight months later, I was arrested. The Word told me I could not serve two masters, but I ignored the truth: God can heal. The night of my arrest I asked God to remove my alcoholism and He did—right on the spot. I've never wanted to drink since. During my incarceration, I learned how to pray, how to search the Word, and how to spend time in the presence of God. I've been writing stories since I was a small child. Writing is a refuge. My story in this book reflects the pain of separation, the strain on communication, and deep remorse and regret.

Patrick Stephens

I was born and raised in Brooklyn, the first-born son of Jamaican parents. I have served twelve years of a twenty-five-to-life sentence as a first-time offender. I have a wide array of interests—from sports and astrology to writing and correspondence chess—but I particularly like psychology. Currently, I serve in a supervisory capacity in several organizations and programs and am an active peer educator for HIV/AIDS, hepatitis, influenza, and smoking cessation. One of my goals is to obtain a master's degree in social work and to work with at-risk children upon my release. A clear turning point in my life was the birth of my son, but the one person who continues to make a significant difference in my life is my mother. She has always helped me be the best I can be. To be worthy of her adoration has been a central focus for me.

Joel Williams

I am a Shoshone-Paiute Native American who hails from Upland, a small town in the foothills of southern California. When I was a young man, I killed the father who had abused me through my childhood and adolescence. I have served twenty-four years of a twenty-seven-to-life sentence. Depending on how many people you asked the question, "Who is Joel Williams?" you'd get as many different answers. Some might say, "He's a quiet and lonesome guy." Others would say, "He's full of it!" A few with long memories might add: "He was a drunken hell-raiser." But those who know me today know that, though I've taken some gut shots from life and have pitched a few myself, I'm working toward some kind of salvation. I play the guitar, design pop-up cards, and continue to write. Some day "in the future" I hope to get paroled and, who knows, maybe even meet a gal.

Editors' Bios

S heila R. Rule is founder of Resilience Multimedia, a publishing company that seeks to present a fairer image of the incarcerated, the formerly incarcerated, and their loved ones. A journalist at *The New York Times* for more than thirty years before retiring from that newspaper, she was led to publishing by her love of books and her respect for the power of stories.

Marsha R. Rule (Marsha R. Leslie) is a writer and editor for UW Medicine, University of Washington, Seattle. She edited *The Single Mother's Companion: Essays and Stories by Women* (Seal Press, 1994) and contributed to *The Black Womens' Health Book* (Seal Press, 1990, 1994). She lives in Seattle.

Order Form

Ordering Method:

Telephone: Call 877-267-2303 toll free.
Have your credit card ready.

Email: *resiliencemultimedia@verizon.net*

Postal: Resilience Multimedia, Dept. B,
511 Avenue of the Americas, Suite 525
New York, NY 10011

Online: *www.thinkoutsidethecell.org*

All books are $14.95 plus shipping:
$3.50 (book rate; delivery speed varies)
$5.75 (priority mail; approx. 1–3 days)

New York residents, please add 8.875% sales tax.
Discount schedule for bulk orders is available upon request.

Number of Copies Requested:

_____ *Love Lives Here, Too: Real-Life Stories about Prison Marriages and Relationships*

_____ *Counting the Years: Real-Life Stories about Waiting for Loved Ones to Return Home from Prison*

_____ *The Hard Journey Home: Real-Life Stories about Reentering Society after Incarceration*

_____ *Think Outside the Cell: An Entrepreneur's Guide for the Incarcerated and Formerly Incarcerated*

Name: _____

Address: _____

City: _____ State: _____ Zip: _____

Daytime phone: _____

Email address: _____

Payment: ❑ Check payable to Resilience Multimedia

❑ Credit card: ❑ Visa ❑ MasterCard ❑ Amex ❑ Discover

Card number: _____ Exp. Date: _____

Name on card: _____